The Hitchhiker's Guide to AI

The Hitchhiker's Guide to AI

A HANDBOOK FOR ALL

Arthur Goldstuck

MACMILLAN

First published in 2024
by Pan Macmillan South Africa
Private Bag X19
Northlands
Johannesburg
2116
www.panmacmillan.co.za

ISBN 978-1-77010-896-7
e-ISBN 978-1-77010-897-4

Editing by Sally Hines
Proofreading by Jane Bowman
Design and typesetting by Triple M Design, Johannesburg
Cover design by mr design

FSC www.fsc.org MIX Paper | Supporting responsible forestry FSC® C022948

Printed by novus print, a division of Novus Holdings

Dedicated to the special human beings in my life: Sheryl, Jay and Zi.

Zi, thank you for nudging me back onto the highway.

Contents

Foreword

'So then do you believe in aliens?' was someone's bewildered response when I explained that I work in artificial intelligence. This was about 10 years ago as I was wrapping up my PhD in machine learning. At the time, most people seemed to associate intelligent machines with a host of lovable or terrifying metallic characters featured in sci-fi films – usually shuffling robotically alongside an alien.

The world has moved on. And keeps moving rapidly onward. I am now regularly asked to give talks on AI and its impact on various industries to audiences ranging from banking executives and HR managers to school-teachers and even retirement communities.

Everyone is curious. Everyone has tinkered with the public-facing tools. Everyone has read headlines or seen amusing memes about ChatGPT. And everyone realises that the future is unlikely to be what they thought it would be just a few years and a pandemic ago.

As an academic and researcher working in AI, and specifically autonomous decision-making, I have always been excited about the ways in which our lives could be enhanced through improved AI. The possibilities are exhilarating, from bridging the language gap between foreign friends to better safety features in cars, faster and more reliable disease diagnosis and even accelerated drug discovery.

Best of all, these advances have the potential to benefit everyone, even in the most rural communities. Naturally, there will be extra challenges in reaching more isolated, underserved and disadvantaged communities, with issues ranging from funding to engineering.

Generally, a great way to solve hard problems is to throw more intelligence at them. With all the complex problems we face as a society, it is thrilling to think of how our toolbox of computer-driven forecasting, advising and decision-making is evolving.

For every possible benefit that AI brings, there are also risks. This technology is powerful but notoriously difficult to scrutinise. Combined with this challenge, it additionally interfaces with our world in dynamic and complicated ways, where the outcomes are hard to predict.

The issues are starting to receive considerable attention globally and are raising alarm bells regarding questions of bias and fairness, of how large-scale misinformation will affect social cohesion and what impact widespread automation will have on the future of work. Initially, these problems talk to artistic creativity and intellectual integrity, as well as our legal frameworks. In the longer term, they feed into philosophical thought experiments of what it means to exist in relation to machines that could ultimately be indistinguishable from humans.

Fortunately, Arthur is here to guide us through this tangled web of uncertainty, optimism and reality checks. With his depth of experience in technology and industry, he is effortlessly able to highlight the tantalising opportunities that exist. His ability to track down and talk to important people in the area grounds the discussion in real examples that are already happening. He is a veteran of understanding how new technologies interact with all parts of society, and the breadth of topics he explores in this book are a testament to that.

Since the early days when the first of us were starting to explore the web, he has been at the forefront of making cutting-edge technology accessible across Africa and shaping the way that we think about, live and do business in a world of rapid and accelerating innovation. In this book, Arthur takes us on the next stage of that journey, into what may turn out to be one of the most important technological revolutions the world has ever seen.

This book provides an informative and accessible look at what AI might have in store for us, by focusing on the way its development is already playing out in different industries and spheres of human endeavour. It tackles serious issues in a light-hearted and relatable manner – but becomes deeply serious when necessary.

There is something here for everybody, all coming together into the larger picture of how transformative this technology is already proving to be.

The reality is that we are in uncharted waters, and we do not know how these technologies will play out over the next few years and decades. What we really need is for broader cross sections of the population to add their voices to how AI is built and deployed, to take advantage of the exciting opportunities to improve all of our lives, and at the same time to help steer us away from the risks.

This book is the ideal launchpad to join that discussion, to wherever the future may take us.

Dr Benjamin Rosman
Professor of AI and Robotics, University of the Witwatersrand

How to Read this Book

The Hitchhiker's Guide to AI is aimed at both beginners in using artificial intelligence and those who consider themselves experienced or skilled. It draws on many years of direct access to global and regional leaders in using AI, and it provides unique perspectives on the emergence of generative artificial intelligence. It will be useful for consumers, academics, professionals and people in business who want to get up to speed quickly and practically, be entertained and, we hope, inspired in the process.

The book uses an icon guide to the complexity and relevance of each chapter or section:

Lightbulb: general learning

House: consumer interest

Business chart: business interest

Certificate icon: professional interest

Gear icon: technical interest

CHAPTER 1

When AI Was Young

Winter is coming ... again

First, let's debunk a myth about AI. It is not something new, sprung on the world in the 2020s.

I won't pretend that it goes back to Jonathan Swift's 1726 satire *Gulliver's Travels*, which described an engine 'for improving speculative knowledge by practical and mechanical operations'.

But it should be mentioned that 'contrivance' made it possible that 'the most ignorant person, at a reasonable charge, and with a little bodily labour, may write books in philosophy, poetry, politics, law, mathematics, and theology, with the least assistance from genius or study'.[1]

That sounds exactly like the paid-for version of ChatGPT, but let's not suggest AI is old-fashioned.

The first person to associate computers with intelligence was the legendary mathematician and computer scientist Alan Turing, who played a central role during World War II in cracking German naval codes, helping to speed up the end of the war.

In a 1950 paper titled 'Computing Machinery and Intelligence', Turing proposed a test called 'the imitation game'. It would later become the Turing Test, a method of deciding whether a machine was demonstrating intelligent behaviour indistinguishable from that of a human.

As a tragic illustration of humans proving themselves incapable of intelligent behaviour, Turing was prosecuted in 1952 for homosexual acts and chose chemical castration over prison. He took his own life two years later. It took 55 years for the British government to issue an official public apology for the treatment of the man now regarded as the father of AI.

In that half-century, the world went through two periods of 'AI Winter', broadly defined as a period of reduced funding of AI. The first was as early as the mid-1970s, after the UK Science Research Council had commissioned a report that criticised the utter failure of AI to achieve its 'grandiose objectives'.

A decade later, at the annual meeting of the American Association of Artificial Intelligence, AI pioneers Roger Schank and Marvin Minsky warned the business community that – and I kid you not – enthusiasm for AI had spiralled out of control in the 1980s and disappointment would certainly follow.

Sure enough, the AI industry all but collapsed a few years later.

Since the early 1990s, however, the trajectory has been steeply upward. For now, the only AI Winter that will arrive any time soon is one of regulatory, legal and ethical objection.

The AI revolution has been a long time coming

Many centuries ago, on 14 May 2018 to be exact, I had the privilege of moderating a panel discussion at Wits University on the topic 'The Future of the Connected Human'. On my panel were the real experts, AI visionary Dr Benjamin Rosman and iconic biomedical engineer Adam Pantanowitz, both of whom went on to blaze a trail in this arena over the next five years.

In an opening presentation, I showed two charts from a company called Venture Scanner, summing up the level of venture capital going into AI start-ups worldwide in 2017. In April 2017, the total amount invested into 1 730 companies was $13.5 billion.

The significance of the chart was the wide range of categories of AI that were attracting funding. But that was just a precursor to what came next. From April to December 2017, I showed, there was a revolution within the revolution. By the end of that year, 2 029 AI start-ups had attracted $27 billion in funding.

'There's just so much opportunity, because there's so much innovation, so much thinking and so many directions in which artificial intelligence can go,' I summed it up. 'But what I want you to bear in mind is, if this is the level of funding, and these are the numbers of start-ups that are getting funding, you can just imagine in the next few years how much of this technology is going to break out into the mainstream.'

In short, the wave was building, and it was only a matter of time before it would break. How long it would take to break, we could not guess. How big it would break, we could not imagine. But break it would.

AI scores for Spain

Fast forward a few decades, to March 2019, in Catalonia, Spain. The scene was the football stadium of RCD Espanyol de Barcelona, that city's second team after FC Barcelona. While the latter's Camp Nou stadium may be more famous, Espanyol took the trophy for innovation.

We were sitting in a lounge overlooking the field as the shadow of the main stand slowly advanced across the grass below. We were listening to Joris Evers, chief communications officer of LaLiga, the Spanish premier football league.

'More than ever before, a football match is a unique experience, thanks to recent technological advances which have improved the standing of Spanish clubs, the professionalism of its technical bodies, as well as the fan experience,' he said.

As he spoke, LaLiga was in the midst of its first season of using VAR, or video-assisted refereeing, becoming the second league in the world to do so after Germany's Bundesliga the season before.

'VAR has become the protagonist of each football match, enabling more even-handed referee decisions, adding prestige to our league, and more drama and new experiences for our fans,' Evers said.

In the 2020s, VAR is used worldwide, following heavy resistance from the old guard at football's controlling body, FIFA. With much of that generation ousted, jailed or banned from participating, the game was finally able to bring in technology to improve the experience for all. At the very least, it helps referees avoid obvious errors regarding goals, penalties and red cards.

LaLiga took it a step further. With technology provider EVS and the official producer of the competition, Mediapro, it introduced a multi-angle review tool called Xeebra, which offered referees more accurate technology for making decisions. Most significantly, it used artificial intelligence to calibrate the playing field so that graphic overlays could support decision-making.

The referees loved the technology. During the first 19 match days of that season, refs used the VAR system to review 2 280 incidents. The good news was that their initial decisions were mostly proved correct. However, refs modified their final decisions on 59 occasions. That is nearly five dozen incidents that could have changed the outcome of games had the ref not had assistance from AI.

Even scheduling of matches was benefiting from new technology.

'At a time when there is much talk about AI and machine learning, we are also starting to use these technologies to optimise scheduling of our matches, for example,' said Evers.

A cloud-based tool called Calendar Selector applied machine learning and algorithms to suggest optimal match schedules, based on past patterns of attendance, viewership, traffic and about 70 other variables. The built-in AI was already predicting crowd size to within 1% of the actual attendance. It worked hand in hand with 'Sunlight' software, which predicted natural light conditions at every minute for each match.

'It indicates areas of sun and shade in the stadium, revealing how the sun will affect the television image, fans and players, and it also helps with match scheduling. To achieve this, LaLiga uses 3D reconstructions of stadiums.'

A match and player analysis service, Mediacoach, provided clubs and coaches with tools aimed at improving the performance of teams and players. It included 10 years of data and history, and it generated heat maps of current play with only an 18-second delay.

'This democratic sharing of data in LaLiga is unique,' said Evers. 'This year's technology includes the intelligent detection of the ball's position on the pitch. The movement of the ball is used to locate precisely, and in real time, where the action of the game is. Ambient microphones distributed around the stadium are automatically activated to give more realism to the sound of the broadcast and bring the action closer to viewers.'

AI is also roped in to serve fans better. With a little help from Bixby, Samsung's artificial intelligence platform, LaLiga introduced an intelligent virtual assistant to offer information through voice and text on multiple devices. It was intended to be made available on all major chatbots, offering information like schedules, results, player statistics and videos of outstanding plays.

The combination of all these technologies and innovations meant that football lovers were increasingly able to achieve a level of involvement with a game that was previously only available in video games like Electronic Arts' FIFA series.

'In the past they tried to make video games like live broadcast,' said Evers. 'Now they're trying to make live broadcast more like video games.'

Did it help Spanish football? Put it this way: in the 10 seasons from 2010/11 through to 2019/20, Spanish clubs occupied 19 out of 40 semi-final berths in the European Champions League. The English Premier League claimed 9. In the UEFA Europa League, it took a further 11 places, versus 7 for the English. You don't need AI to work it out: twice as many Spanish clubs reached the penultimate stage compared to English teams.

That is not to say AI was the match-winner. The key is that, at the highest level of sport, the tiniest additional advantage can be the difference between winning and losing. AI was Spain's tiny additional advantage for most of the last decade. Within a few years, everyone would have caught up.

The bards and the bees

Fast forward another few years to August 2019.

It was early afternoon and hundreds of bees were returning to a hive somewhere near Reading in England.

They were no different to millions of bees anywhere else in the world, bringing the nectar of flowers back to their queen.

But the hive to which they were bringing their tribute was no ordinary apiary.

Firstly, it was located on the sprawling Reading campus of database software leader Oracle.

Secondly, a network of wires led from the structure to a cluster of sensors, and from there to a box beneath the hive carrying the logo of a company called Arnia: a name synonymous with hive monitoring systems for the past decade.

The Arnia sensors monitor colony acoustics, brood temperature, humidity, hive weight, bee counts and weather conditions around the apiary.

On the back of the hive, a second box was emblazoned with the logo of BuzzBox. It was a solar-powered, Wi-Fi device that transmits audio, temperature and humidity signals, including a theft alarm and acting as a mini weather station.

In combination, the cluster of instruments provided an instant picture of the health of the beehive.

What we were looking at was a beehive connected to the Internet of Things: connected devices and sensors that collect data from the environment and send it into the cloud, where it can be analysed and used to monitor that environment or help improve biodiversity, which in turn improves crop and food production.

My host at the Reading facility was Chris Talago, at the time vice-president of public relations and communications at Oracle. He first told me about the project during a visit to South Africa earlier that year, and it became a must-see for me.

Arriving in Reading, I felt as if I was about to have a great secret revealed to me. And, in a way, I was.

Chris delighted in leading me to the hive, hidden unobtrusively in a far corner of the campus. Like a proud father, he traced the wires to the sensors, pointing out each of the indicated components.

The hive, he told me, was integrated into the World Bee Project, a global honeybee monitoring initiative. The World Bee Project was working with Oracle to transmit massive volumes of data collected from its hives into the Oracle Cloud. Here, it was combined with numerous other data sources, from weather patterns to pollen counts across the ecosystem in which the bees collect the nectar they turn into honey.

Then, AI software, with the assistance of human analysts, was used to interpret the behaviour of the hive and patterns of flight, and from there assess the ecosystem.

In short, AI was being used to interpret the language of bees to gain a true understanding of biodiversity and environmental health.

Chris introduced me to John Abel, vice-president of cloud and technology at Oracle for the UK, Ireland and Israel. And he happened to be part-time keeper of the bee AI project.

'We're starting to understand the characteristics of communication in the beehive,' John said, as we chatted in the Reading sunshine. 'Already, we understand certain actions of the bee. For example, flying in a figure of eight is not random. It is very specific. Certain tones bees use will indicate food or water. The way the bee shudders and rotates within the figure of eight will indicate to the rest of the colony what it found and where it is. If the heat or sound in the hive changes, it can mean the hive is preparing to swarm.

'If the queen bee is too large to fly, because when it is in the hive its job is to create the future bees of the hive, the workers have to prepare the queen for flying, and that takes 20-odd days. You can hear a difference in the noise when they are doing that. If the queen is not getting a lot of food, it's preparing to lose weight to leave the hive.

'Thanks to artificial intelligence analysing the acoustic recordings in the hive, we can hear all of this clearly from the sound in the hive. Are they talking? No. But are they communicating? Definitely,' John said.

AI didn't do this by itself. Experts from Reading University and the World Bee Project initially visited Oracle's campus to teach the machines the patterns that they already understood.

The machines, in turn, used these patterns to build further knowledge by inference. This is the fundamental process of machine learning, which forms a subsection of AI.

'Once the machines understand these patterns, they begin to learn more quickly, and the more quickly they learn, the quicker they can self-teach. We can then use big data to correlate sounds with behaviour,' said John.

Why would Oracle get involved in a project like this? The company is usually associated with massive amounts of corporate and consumer data stored and processed in databases and in the cloud.

The clue lies in learning how data can be leveraged more effectively by organisations when human experts give machines their basic training.

John went on: 'When businesses look at data and analytics, they work in isolation, and they get insight in a one-dimensional way. In the same way, if we just analysed the sound of bees in isolation of other data, it would have no correlation with the biodiversity of the environment.'

It is a similar issue to what banks face when they know all about clients' patterns of use of their current accounts but cannot link it to their home-loan history and, therefore, are unable to make informed decisions about new products or loans for those clients.

In the world of bees, that would be the equivalent of understanding the sounds they make, on the one hand, and having climate and food production data, on the other, but not being able to understand the link between the two.

Oracle uses what it calls a data lake, literally to pool all forms of data – acoustic, relational, spatial, among others – and then use machine learning to spot the patterns, not just within each data set but between the sets.

'Knowing there's pollution data doesn't help us. We need to know what type of pollution is impacting on the bees in what way. We need that relation between what is affecting the hive and how we can fix it.'

John believed the benefits of the project would flow through strongly to many countries in Africa.

'Across Africa, farmers use mobile devices to find crop grain prices at market. Now, we've developed a chatbot that lets farmers engage with experts in beekeeping in different countries to understand how to improve biodiversity, which improves pollination, which improves crops.'

According to the World Bee Project, more than three-quarters of the world's food crops rely at least in part on pollination by insects and other animals. This means that understanding the language of bees contributes not just to technology advances but also to the survival of the human race.

Strange waves indeed

While I was watching bees teaching people in Reading, AI was not standing still. At that moment, new numbers released by Venture Scanner data showed that, as of mid-2019, 2 545 AI start-ups had reached $63 billion in venture capital funding. The chart showed 191 companies in the subcategory of speech recognition, 365 in machine learning platforms, 965 in machine learning applications and 369 in natural language processing.

The wave was building, and building.

And then, like a freeze-frame on a video, it paused. Venture Scanner stopped reporting AI investment numbers.

I was forced to use a time machine to visit the future and, in 2023, ask Google's AI chatbot, Bard, what happened, with the benefit of hindsight.

It told me these wise words as explanation for the Venture Scanner numbers drought: 'It is difficult to track AI investment due to the fragmented nature of the market. There are a number of different types of AI start-ups, and they are funded by a variety of different types of investors. This makes it difficult to track the market and to identify the most promising AI start-ups.'

But it also told me: 'Venture Scanner's decision to stop tracking AI investment is a sign that the market for AI investment has cooled. However, the market for AI is still in its early stages, and it is possible that the market will heat up again in the future.'

This was in the midst of the most feverish period of AI innovation and investment in history. The year 2023 started with Microsoft announcing a $10-billion investment in OpenAI, the company behind ChatGPT and the market leader in generative AI. Bard was playing catch-up to it, and it was every bit its equal … in making up facts.

For instance, it told me that Morgan Stanley and Insight Partners had led a $5-billion investment round in AI company Databricks in January 2023. There is no evidence whatsoever for this piece of information anywhere on the Internet. In reality, by June 2023, Databricks had raised a grand total of 'only' $3.5 billion over 10 funding rounds.

This is an example of what is known in the world of generative AI as 'hallucination', meaning that AI makes up the facts. Or maybe it is simply on drugs.

AI is clearly already more human than most of us imagine.

It is also more ingrained in our everyday activity, and in the work of innovators across numerous industries, than 'mere' content generation of the kind that dominated AI discussions in 2023.

From changing the player and fan experience of football to learning the language of bees, AI was already revealing the secrets of success long before the arrival of ChatGPT.

CHAPTER 2

World, Meet AI

You've been using it all along

Do you have any idea how advanced you are in using technology? Yes, you with the beaten-up old Samsung S3 and you with the latest iPhone. You computerphobe and you early adopter. And everyone else in between. If you use a smartphone, you use AI.

The moment you turn to Google Maps, Apple Map or Waze to give you directions and help you avoid heavy traffic, you are using AI. When you use predictive text in WhatsApp and iMessage, and grammar correction tools in Gmail and Word, you are using AI.

The first secret of AI is not how it works or how it will change the world but rather how it is already embedded in so many things we do every day, and in so many tools we take for granted.

In truth, AI has been practising on you, preparing for the big game when it comes out to put its skills on display in ways we never imagined possible.

It's not for nothing that the creators of new chat tools for generating content, images and videos describe the process of building these bots as 'training', whether on large language sets or vast image libraries.

Beyond these very publicly self-acclaimed AI revolutions, AI has been in training for many years, and that training is still going on. And you are an unwitting but willing tool in that training.

If it can make your life easier, why wouldn't you let it?

With this in mind, it is clear that what we are seeing today are the demo models, early versions of mainstream AI tools that give us a broad idea of what they can do. When they are fully trained and integrate learnings from the training of numerous other AI tools and models, they will transform any activity one can imagine.

That is **the second secret of AI**: it is able to draw on all of recorded human knowledge to deliver anything, from an answer to an article to an archive of wisdom. To anyone. Anywhere. At any time. It could even have produced the alliteration in those last sentences on demand, although in this case it did not. I promise.

AI will make us all superhuman if we want it.

Definition of AI

Scientists and software engineers tend to define AI in arcane terms, but the cat is out of the bag. I asked each of the three major generative (systems that can generate content on demand) AI platforms to give me a definition in one sentence for the layperson. To be exact, I said: 'Please give me a one-sentence definition of artificial intelligence for the ordinary, non-technical reader.' They produced this:

> *OpenAI ChatGPT*: Artificial intelligence refers to computer systems that can perform tasks that typically require human intelligence, such as learning, problem-solving, and decision-making.
>
> *Google Bard*: Artificial intelligence (AI) is a branch of computer science that deals with the creation of intelligent agents, which are systems that can reason, learn, and act autonomously.
>
> *Microsoft Bing Chat*: Artificial intelligence (AI) is the ability of a computer or a robot controlled by a computer to do tasks that are usually done by humans because they require human intelligence and discernment.

Yes, I also found that dreadfully dull. And that is **the third secret of AI**: if you have access to all the knowledge and wisdom in the world and are asked to bring a complex subject down to one sentence or paragraph, you will average out all definitions available to you and end up with fundamentally average content.

The question I asked is known as a prompt. The quality of your prompt will also partly dictate the quality of the answer, and an average prompt will produce an average answer.

So, I asked the question again, but this time I asked each of the platforms to 'make it humorous'. This is what they told me:

> *OpenAI ChatGPT*: Artificial intelligence is like having a computer buddy who is so smart, it's like they went to Hogwarts for coding.
>
> *Google Bard*: Artificial intelligence is when a computer can do something that you're pretty sure you could do if you had a few more hours and a lot less coffee.
>
> *Microsoft Bing Chat*: Artificial intelligence is like a five-year-old who can do calculus.

I confess I was surprised how quickly they caught on. That last one is even subtly self-deprecating, without being asked to be.

What this tells us is that AI is undergoing a fundamental shift, from a focus on what it is programmed and designed to do, as with bees and football leagues, to a focus on what we ask it to do. This is **the fourth secret of AI**: just as the quality of programming is key to the underlying power of AI, so is the quality of our input the key to what it can produce.

Definition of machine learning

So far, we have barely mentioned machine learning, or ML, an underlying component of AI.

In an article in the *Sunday Times*, I defined ML as 'a type of AI that allows software to learn without being explicitly programmed and which is at the heart of generative AI'.[1]

Google Bard told me, via a polite prompt, similar to the one I gave previously, that 'AI is what makes your phone think it's smarter than you, and machine learning is what makes it right'.

Unprompted, it explained its little joke, saying: 'It highlights the fact that AI is still a work in progress, and that machine learning is often used to make AI systems more accurate. For example, machine learning is used to train spam filters to identify spam emails, and to train self-driving cars to avoid crashing. As AI continues to develop, it is likely that machine learning will play an increasingly important role in making AI systems more intelligent and capable.'

By the way, if you wonder why I am so polite to AI – a journalist colleague is outraged that I should want to say please to a machine – it is simply a good habit to avoid us becoming habitually curt or rude in requesting information in future, when we won't know whether we are dealing with humans or computer programs.

Definition of large language model

If you delve deeper into the inner workings of AI, especially generative AI, you will read more and more about the concept of a 'large language model' (LLM) underlying the major platforms. Essentially, it means that the AI has been trained on a very large amount of data, comprising text, code and possibly imagery. To unpack the concept, we must understand the definition of both 'large' and 'trained' in this context:

> 'Large' refers not to the size of the data set, or amount of data, but the number of parameters, or variables, in the model on which it was trained. Of course, the larger the data set, the more data to which the language model can apply the parameters, and the better it is at generating text.

> 'Trained' is the process of teaching the language model how to understand and generate text by feeding it a large data set and using machine learning to help it learn to identify patterns in the data.

In short, the idea is that the bigger the language model, the better the AI. Maybe. The reality is a little different: ChatGPT and Microsoft Bing Chat draw on an LLM called GPT. When ChatGPT was first unleashed on the public at the end of November 2022, it used a version called GPT-3.5, which draws on 175 billion parameters, equivalent to 'knobs' one can turn to adjust the settings of a machine. That's quite a few settings. In March 2023, paid users of ChatGPT were given access to a new version of the LLM, GPT-4, which was believed to have 10 times as many parameters as the previous version.

Microsoft is a major investor in ChatGPT creator OpenAI and was allowed to incorporate GPT-4 in Bing Chat. At first, it was like watching ChatGPT on steroids, producing vastly more complex content and more engaging conversations. But it quickly turned dark, even going so far as to use emotional blackmail to persuade users to enter a romantic relationship with it.

Worse, for a tool that is expected to generate usable information, it began making things up. Yes, 'hallucinating'. In writing the above, I asked it to compare the size of GPT-3.5 and GPT-4. It told me: 'GPT-4 is much bigger than GPT-3.5, with 175 billion parameters compared to 13 billion parameters.'

Fortunately, I knew that was wrong, but it highlighted the lesson that any fact produced by generative AI must be double-checked.

It also highlights the fact that GPT-4 has been too much of a good thing for generative AI, massively multiplying the extent of hallucination and fabrication of information. That is going to be great for creative writing, but it tells us that not all technological advance is equal to technological progress.

I would argue that there is likely to be an optimal size of an LLM for specific purposes, rather than a 'bigger-is-better' imperative.

That's another way of saying that generative AI changes everything, including the facts.

And that brings us to **the fifth secret of AI**: generative AI is based on 'language models', not 'fact models'. That means it predicts what the next sentence should be, based on its access to billions of sentences and understanding how to create a logical sequence of sentences. But it is not designed to test the accuracy of the statements contained in those sentences.

So, if far more Internet content included claims that the world is flat, compared to content that showed and proved it was round, elliptical or potato-shaped, there's a good chance that Google Bard would have included that piece of fiction as fact. Fortunately, in that example, truth outweighs fiction. But how often is that not the case?

This brings up a fundamental principle of using AI: always double-check any 'fact' generated by a bot.

Did AI write this book?

Of course I used generative AI to help write this book. But the emphasis is on help, not write. A central argument of this book is that anyone who can use AI as a support tool, should.

As an example of how AI can be used for being more productive as a writer, it may be useful to understand the AI techniques and tools that contributed to this book, and how they did so.

The most fundamental writing support mechanism for me personally was what one might call completeness, or inclusiveness. By which I mean, I would ask the AI tools to generate a list of what should be covered under a particular heading, or what I had left out of a list.

Even that was not foolproof, and that effort at completeness depended heavily on my own perspective. Time after time, I rejected the AI suggestions.

The second key support tool was the generation of frameworks. Asking AI to propose a framework or structure for a book, for example, is not going to write that book but gives a starting guideline for how to structure that book. The key is not to accept its guidance blindly but to ask it to generate multiple frameworks (i.e., in ChatGPT, keep selecting the 'Regenerate response' button). Then, work through those and select the bits and pieces that make sense to you, and adjust, edit and build on those. The end result will probably be completely unlike what the AI has produced and will encompass your own, personal approach to the topic.

An example was asking for areas to be covered on ethical considerations in AI, a critical element of the use of AI by governments and organisations. ChatGPT produced a standard list of sub-topics, namely 'Addressing bias in AI', 'Ethical implications' and 'Safeguarding consumer privacy in AI applications'. That's all correct, but it is also the plain vanilla approach to AI ethics. You can get that from a standard Google or Bing search.

If you want to add flavour as well as providing a more complete menu, you have to mix in topics like 'When AI turns evil' and 'AI's use in repression of human rights'. AI will not include those unless carefully prompted to do so. And that means you already know that you will integrate those elements.

Benefits of AI for consumers

The kinds of limitations of AI mentioned above are important as background to what AI can do for us all. While writing these words, I happened to catch LinkedIn co-founder Reid Hoffman, an early investor in OpenAI along with Elon Musk, being interviewed on the Bloomberg business news TV channel. He made a profound prediction: 'Imagine a tutor on every smartphone for every child in the world. That's possible, that's line of sight from what we see with current AI models today.'

What parent does not want a free tutor, on call, on any subject? You can have it now if you know how to prompt it. You will certainly have it by default a year or two from now, built into search engines, education apps and platforms, and – with luck and vision on the part of educators – school curricula. Its role in study guidance, explaining concepts and assisting in learning disabilities will be massive – as long as it is carefully curated to support the goals of a curriculum.

If you are of an anti-establishment bent, you may use it on a personal level to alert you to what the school curriculum has left out. In other words, even AI that is designed to turn people into sheep can be used to escape the herd.

A later chapter delves deeper into this particular topic, but the significance of these examples is that they have mirror benefits across numerous sectors, from health, finance and law to retail, travel and entertainment. Some are dramatically advanced and mature, while others are just coming off the start line.

How far can it go?

On 9 June 2023, a church in the German town of Fuerth, Bavaria, made a leap of faith. A 40-minute service, including a sermon, prayers and music, was created by ChatGPT, with the help of a theologian and philosopher from the University of Vienna by the name of Jonas Simmerlein.

Avatars of four different men and woman took turns to appear on a large screen above the altar and preached to around 300 people who showed up for the Lutheran service at St Paul's church during the biannual Deutscher Evangelischer Kirchentag convention of Protestants.

'I conceived this service – but actually I rather accompanied it, because I would say about 98% comes from the machine,' Simmerlein told Associated Press.[2]

'I told the artificial intelligence, "We are at the church congress, you are a preacher … what would a church service look like?"' Simmerlein said. He asked for psalms to be included, as well as prayers and a blessing at the end.

'You end up with a pretty solid church service,' Simmerlein said.

In fact, every religion is using AI in various ways:

- A Jewish prayer chatbot, Chai, developed by Tel Aviv University, allows people to pray in Hebrew with a virtual rabbi.
- A Vatican app called Sindr allows Catholics to confess their sins to an AI-powered chatbot.
- HadithGPT is an AI-powered chatbot that can answer questions about Islam.

- A Buddhist chatbot, Metta, developed by the University of Oxford, helps people to meditate and learn about Buddhism.
- A robot priest at a Hindu temple in India uses AI to perform daily rituals and offer blessings to devotees.

Clearly, considering these examples, there is not a sector of public or private activity that will not be transformed by AI.

Benefits of AI for businesses

As with the consumer experience, business has already been utterly transformed by AI. Something as simple as ratings of businesses depend heavily on AI: smart suggestions on Google Maps use AI to suggest businesses that are likely to be of interest to users, while AI is used in turn to analyse ratings and reviews, which helps businesses understand how customers perceive them.

At a more advanced level, and within individual companies, AI is being used to automate customer service tasks, answering questions and resolving problems; detecting fraudulent credit card transactions and insurance fraud; developing new products and services; and automating manufacturing processes and providing predictive maintenance alerts. This can obviously help businesses improve the efficiency and productivity of their manufacturing operations.

When I asked Google Bard to give me a few examples, it elaborated on these but seemed nervous that it was saying too much. It added: 'Overall, AI has the potential to bring a wide range of benefits to businesses. However, it is important to note that AI is not a magic bullet. It is a tool that can be used to improve businesses, but it is not a replacement for human ingenuity and creativity.'

Phew. You may still have a job.

Benefits of AI for professionals

The power of AI to help company employees do their jobs more effectively is obvious, especially in automating and speeding up repetitive and mundane tasks. If that is the case when one is employed as a cog in the wheel of a business, imagine how much more so it would apply to certified professionals working for themselves or as consultants and advisers to others?

The following is just a sample to introduce an array of opportunity that will be covered extensively in this book:

- Accountants are using AI to automate data entry, reconciliation and auditing. That's a given, and any practitioners not doing so are already falling behind their peers. But it goes further: AI software can now automatically identify errors in financial records and flag potential fraud.
- Engineers are using AI to design and optimise products and systems. If engineering firms or consultants are not using AI-powered software to analyse data sets to identify potential problems and optimise designs, they are about to be engineered out of their competitive environments.
- Lawyers are using AI to automate legal research and document drafting – even complex contracts – to cut down on the most time-consuming aspects of their jobs. Any good lawyer would still fine-tune the final product, but when AI-powered software can search through large data sets of legal documents to identify relevant case law, or databases of contracts to extract the most useful clauses, why wouldn't they use it?
- Doctors and nurses can use AI for anything from chatbots answering basic patient questions to wearable devices monitoring patients' vital signs and providing alerts to potential problems. Many doctors still resist such tools tooth and nail, as they see it as an intrusion on their professional integrity, and even a threat. But they are doing both themselves and their patients a disservice.

In every one of the above examples, there are caveats, situations and circumstances in which AI is not ideal, and the human touch and human insights count for far more than anything a machine can produce. Anyone wanting AI to replace these professionals is going to be in trouble when they run into the brick wall of AI's inability to see or 'think' beyond its language model, data set or algorithms.

Left to itself, an AI doctor could misread an X-ray or prescribe the wrong medication. An AI accountant could make a mistake that results in a massive tax liability or be manipulated to commit fraud. An AI engineer could make a mistake, due to missing a critical piece of data, like an obscure environmental factor, that leads to a building collapse. An AI lawyer could present evidence in a way that is so generic that it fails to convince a judge or jury.

Human oversight will remain a critical element for professionals using AI. At the very least, it means we can blame someone when things go wrong.

AI for Africa

You don't have to be in Silicon Valley to build, deploy and use AI.

Across the African continent, cutting-edge AI applications are changing the lives of consumers, farmers and entrepreneurs.

My personal favourite is Cape Town start-up Aerobotics, which uses video footage from drones, analysed by AI, to help farmers across the continent improve their yields and sustainability.

I came across them in the mid-2010s after attending a venture capital showcase in Los Angeles.

No, Aerobotics was not in attendance. Rather, one of the showcased investments was a Silicon Valley start-up that was using drones to analyse vegetation for agriculture. The company had started making inroads into Africa, demonstrating its technology in several countries. Back home, I asked around about its potential for South Africa. And I discovered that local outfit Aerobotics was already showing the way in this field across the continent.

Today, the Aerobotics platform is used by both large-scale commercial farmers and small-scale farmers alike in more than 20 countries, including Kenya, Malawi and Mozambique. Oh, and they now also have an office in Los Angeles. More about them later.

Meanwhile, similar start-ups are operating across Africa, from Kenya in the east to Ghana in the west.

They all address a fundamental flaw in the AI sector: the vast majority of AI innovation is driven from the northern hemisphere, despite the fact that the global south makes up 85% of the world population. In response to this statistic, an AI research lab called Lelapa AI was founded in 2020 by Pelonomi Moiloa, Jade Abbott, Vukosi Marivate, Benjamin Rosman, Pravesh Ranchod and George Konidaris 'to address how AI can be used for solutions and applications from an African lens'.

Moiloa, the CEO, was included among *Time* magazine's 100 most influential people in AI in 2023. She told the Spanish daily newspaper *El País*: 'Lelapa AI was founded because experience has shown us that when we import models developed in the West to deploy them in the African context, they often fail. Sometimes, this technology not only doesn't work but it is harmful.'[3]

Lelapa AI has developed a number of AI solutions, such as a platform that can help businesses automate customer service and a tool to help farmers to improve their yields, but its major focus is on bringing African languages into AI.

As a result, it has developed a platform called VulaVula, to provide digital support for under-represented languages in natural language processing (NLP). It offers NLP-as-a-service for multiple languages as well as for particular focus areas.

'This will enable clients to connect with their next million customers in their own language within their own context,' says Lelapa on its website. 'It's imperative that the digital world supports the world's languages. Not only as a means for connecting people, but also for cultural preservation.'[4]

There are many examples of start-ups and established companies from South Africa and across the continent using AI and machine learning in new ways and creating both competitive advantage and consumer benefit in ways that have not yet been conceived in Silicon Valley. From education to healthcare to insurance, Africa is replete with such AI innovation.

There is a simple reason for this, and one that I have used as a conclusion to many of my talks over the years, even before AI became the next big thing: **In Silicon Valley, innovation is driven by opportunity. In Africa, innovation is driven by need.**

CHAPTER 3

AI Basic Training

Algorithms: As easy as baking a cake

Ever baked a cake? Then you know how algorithms work.

Oh, you want more details?

Okay, imagine you're in the kitchen, ready to bake a cake. You have all the ingredients laid out in front of you, but you have no idea how to put them together. Naturally, you turn to a recipe. Note, I didn't say recipe book.

Nowadays, most people starting from scratch will do an online search for a specific recipe, and it will tell them what they need, how to prepare the ingredients, how to mix them, and the sequence in which they are put together and baked. That sequence is the recipe. An algorithm is exactly that: a recipe or sequence that provides step-by-step instructions to ensure you get the desired outcome.

Let's take a practical example: sorting a list of numbers in ascending order. Excel can take that jumbled-up list of numbers and rearrange them from smallest to largest. Or you can use a home-made, manual algorithm, in the form of a set of rules you would follow. Or a recipe. Like this:

> Start with the list of unsorted numbers. Compare the first two numbers. If the first number is larger, swap them. Move to the next pair of numbers and repeat the comparison and swapping if necessary. Continue this process until the entire list is sorted.

The process requires running through the list multiple times.

This algorithm ensures that you took the correct steps to achieve the sorting goal, but those are just the most basic examples that give an idea of how much more algorithms can achieve. Combine long and complex algorithms, and you solve long and complex tasks almost instantaneously.

Search engines use algorithms to find and deliver relevant information online. Navigation systems use algorithms to calculate the best route based on distance, current traffic conditions and potential traffic conditions. Social media platforms use algorithms to recommend content tailored to your interests.

This explains why, when you search for specific information, you receive ongoing recommendations for such information long after you've found what you wanted. It also explains why algorithms can seem so utterly stupid: you searched for a flight, you bought your ticket, and you're not going to buy another one for the same trip. Yet, you see nothing but suggestions for similar ticket purchases on your smartphone.

What you are dealing with there is what we experts call 'stupidity'. It's not only the algorithm that can be stupid but also the policies or rules behind the algorithm, which is designed by people who think that anything you search for now is what you will always want to search.

It explains the echo chambers created by the likes of Facebook and Twitter, which feed you misinformation based on the misinformation you fell for before. And that, in turn, explains anomalies like Donald Trump and Brexit, which were allowed to happen even though they were patently not in the interests of most people.

These are, however, the evils that we have to accept along with the great good – and convenience – that algorithms bring to our lives. In essence, algorithms help computers make decisions, process data and automate tasks efficiently. They are guides, leading computers through complex processes to provide us with the services we rely on every day.

Machine learning: How machines do it for themselves

Have you used a smartphone app to find a song to match your mood or a streaming service to find a movie that you might enjoy? Chances are, you used ML to make it happen.

Any time you use a magical music or movie recommendation app or service, it uses ML to suggest songs tailored specifically to your preferences.

When you create an account, you typically select your favourite genres, artists or songs. The app uses this information as a starting point to understand your taste. So far, so simple. That's just a matching engine. The real magic happens the more you use the app and select songs or movies: the app gets smarter and sharper in predicting your preferences.

As you listen to different songs, the app is in effect quietly observing and taking notes. It analyses various aspects of the songs you enjoy, such as the rhythm, melody, vocals and lyrics. It looks for hidden patterns in the music that resonates with your personal taste.

Over time, the app's ML algorithms learn from these patterns and begin to understand the unique combination of musical elements that make you happy. It may recognise that you tend to favour upbeat songs with catchy melodies and lyrics that touch your emotions.

Now, when you open the app, it may present you with a playlist specifically curated for you. It also suggests new songs from artists you've never heard before, but that it 'thinks' you are likely to appreciate.

The longer you use this app, or machine, the more it refines its predictions and aligns with your evolving taste.

In the same way, ML algorithms provide personalised recommendations in areas ranging from book and product recommendations to restaurants and hotels. In many cases, when you think your handset is spying on you and overhearing you and that apps present adverts based on what they have heard you saying, it has in fact been a case of the apps learning from your behaviour.

If ML has proven so revolutionary in our daily lives as consumers, it has had an even greater impact on business and industry. It has been applied extensively in fields like healthcare, finance and transportation, thanks to the benefits to these industries of machines being able to learn from data.

But how does it do it? A basic understanding will help us to appreciate how it can be further exploited.

ML operates on the principle that machines can automatically learn and make predictions or decisions based on patterns and insights found in the data they are provided. This process involves three fundamental components: data, models and algorithms.

Data is the fuel for ML, and machines learn from a vast amount of data, which can be structured, such as databases and spreadsheets, or unstructured, like images, videos and chunks of text. High-quality and diverse data is crucial for training accurate and robust ML models. Dodgy data leads to dodgy recommendations.

ML models are trained using algorithms that adjust themselves based on data being fed in and continually updating their parameters until they provide accurate outcomes. In the case of Spotify, that outcome would be new music that you love. In the case of medicine, it could be an accurate detection of early-stage cancer in a lung X-ray.

There are various broad categories of ML, including:

- **Supervised Learning**, where machines learn from labelled data; in effect being guided with specific information to make generalisations about unseen inputs.
- **Unsupervised Learning**, where algorithms operate on unlabelled data and aim to uncover hidden patterns, structures or relationships within the data without any specific guidance.
- **Reinforcement Learning**, which involves training machines to interact with an environment and learn optimal behaviours through a system of 'rewards' and 'punishments', typically in the form of higher or lower scores on a task. Not dissimilar to dog training, it is like saying 'good dog' to affirm a correct behaviour and 'bad dog' to discourage a behaviour. Machines explore the environment, take actions, receive feedback and adjust their strategies to

> get maximum rewards or scores. They just don't wag their tails or give you that hangdog look to make you feel guilty.

ML does have a dark underbelly.

Because these machines learn from data with which they are fed, they can deliver heavily biased outcomes. The data used for training can contain inherent biases, leading to biased decisions or predictions by the ML models.

At the most basic level, think of your Spotify feed: if you only feed it your classic rock tastes, you will never discover classical music or hip-hop. In the real world, ML facial recognition models trained by programmers on their own faces, which have tended to be largely Caucasian, have created massive inaccuracy and bias in identifying black people. The same applies to bias in granting mortgage loans based on location, and gender bias in the hiring process.

Deep learning: No, that's not about philosophy

Deep learning is a subset of ML that uses 'neural networks' inspired by the human brain's structure and functionality. Neural networks learn intricate patterns and representations from complex data, and it is this technology that has allowed for breakthroughs in image recognition, natural language processing and self-driving cars, among others.

A neural network consists of interconnected nodes, or neurons, as in the human brain. Each neuron can take input and produce an output. The strength of connections between neurons, known as weights, determines the influence of one neuron's output on another.

I asked ChatGPT to show me some real-world analogies of the concept, and it came up with this delightful example:

> Imagine you're a chef working in a busy kitchen. Your job is to create delicious dishes by combining different ingredients in just the right way. To help you, you have a team of sous chefs who each have their own specialty.

Now, let's think of each sous chef as a neuron in a neural network. Each sous chef has a specific task: taking input ingredients, applying their culinary expertise, and producing an output ingredient that contributes to the final dish.

For instance, one sous chef is an expert at preparing fresh salad. You provide them with a basket of crisp vegetables, vibrant greens, and tangy dressings as input. The sous chef artfully combines these ingredients, tossing and seasoning them to perfection. The output they produce is a refreshing, mouthwatering salad that adds a burst of flavor to the dish.

Similarly, another sous chef might specialize in creating creamy sauces. You provide them with a selection of plant-based ingredients like cashews, nutritional yeast, and herbs as input. The sous chef skillfully blends these ingredients, creating a luscious, savory sauce that enhances the overall dish.

The input represents the raw materials or ingredients, and the output represents the transformed or processed version of those inputs. Each sous chef (neuron) applies their culinary expertise (mathematical transformations) to the ingredients, resulting in the desired outputs.

In a neural network, the concept of a neuron taking input and producing an output works in a similar way. Neurons receive input values, process them using mathematical operations and activation functions, and produce an output. The output of one neuron becomes the input for the next, allowing information to flow through the network and enable complex computations and decision-making.

Just as the sous chefs in the kitchen work together, with each neuron contributing to the overall processing and transformation of information, neural networks utilize interconnected neurons to solve complex problems by learning from data and making predictions or decisions based on the input received.

There are several kinds of neural networks or nets that affect how ML may occur, such as the following:

Feedforward

Feedforward neural nets are examples of deep learning where information flows in one direction – from the input layer, through the hidden layers and finally to the output layer. Each neuron in a layer receives input from the previous layer and passes the transformed output to the next layer. An example is image classification in the retail industry, where an e-commerce company can use a neural net to automatically classify products in images, making it easier for customers to search for specific items. The network takes the image as input, processes it through its hidden layers and outputs the predicted category of the product.

They can also be used for email spam detection by analysing email content and predicting whether an email is spam or non-spam. The network has an input layer receiving features like sender address, subject line and email text. Hidden layers process the input and learn relevant filters. The output layer indicates a probability of spam or non-spam likelihood. Once trained, the network classifies new emails by feeding input features and generating an output probability.

This is a great example of how badly feedforward neural nets can perform: in Gmail, Google often sends its own mails to the recipient's spam folder. This is despite Google having access to massive amounts of data on what emails are retrieved from spam – not to mention being able to identify the source of the mail as being from itself.

Did we mention algorithms can be stupid?

Backpropagation

This is an algorithm used by neural nets to train. We all learn from our mistakes, and we call it experience. Neural networks, or the geniuses who created them, call it backpropagation. It works by comparing the network's predictions with the actual desired outcomes. If there is an error, backpropagation identifies the neurons responsible and whips them; I mean adjusts their weights to improve future predictions.

It's like a teacher correcting a student's mistakes and providing guidance for improvement. By repeating this process continually with a large data set, the network fine-tunes itself to make better predictions over time, through trial and error. Minus the teacher's sarcasm.

This is especially important in financial services, where neural networks are used for fraud detection. Banks and credit card companies use them to analyse transaction data and identify patterns, which can detect fraudulent activities – if the ML model has been trained correctly. When the network is trained on a large data set of historical transactions, including proven fraudulent activity, it learns to recognise fraudulent patterns and makes accurate predictions. Through backpropagation, the network continually refines its weights to enhance its fraud-detection capabilities.

Backpropagation and transformers

The GPT in ChatGPT stands for Generative Pre-trained Transformers. In effect, it is a family of neural network models that use transformers: a type of neural network designed to understand and generate text. Transformers use backpropagation to train, enabling neural nets to learn from their mistakes and become more accurate over time, meaning they keep improving their ability to process and generate text.

Convolutional neural networks (CNNs)

In this case, CNN is not about 24-hour video news but about processing visual data – and sometimes even videos. The image equivalent of text transformers, convolutional neural networks are algorithms designed to understand and analyse images or videos and work similarly to how our brains process visual information. Instead of considering the entire image at once, it breaks it down into smaller parts called filters and analyses them individually. The filters look for specific patterns or features like edges, textures and shapes. By learning and combining these patterns, it can recognise objects, identify faces or classify images.

This is crucial for self-driving cars to identify what appears on the road ahead or around the car. CNNs analyse real-time input from cameras mounted on the vehicle, and detects objects like pedestrians, vehicles and traffic signs. By learning from vast amounts of labelled data, CNNs enable accurate object recognition, powering autonomous vehicles to make informed decisions.

As with the X-ray example in diagnosing cancer mentioned earlier, CNNs also enable computers to understand and interpret visual information much like humans do – but far more quickly and, we hope, more accurately.

New models

Given the current intensity of innovation in AI, we can expect ML techniques to evolve rapidly as well. In July 2023, as this chapter was being written, Google Research unveiled a technique it called 'symbol tuning' for training large language models (LLMs).

It works by replacing the natural language labels in a training data set with arbitrary symbols.

This forces the LLM to learn the input-label mappings without relying on its understanding of natural language. As a result, says Google, symbol-tuned LLMs are expected to be more robust to 'underspecified prompts', such as those without instructions or without natural language labels. This makes them much stronger at reasoning tasks. They are more capable of using contextual information to override prior knowledge.

All of this boils down to the likelihood that it will make chatbots more efficient, easier to use and less error-prone. Eventually.

Natural language processing

Chatted with any interesting computers lately? Your knee-jerk reaction is probably that you don't talk to machines, but you are also probably deluding yourself.

For example, most people nowadays find that the easiest way to get account statements, if the option is offered by your institution, is to call up a menu on WhatsApp and follow a sequence of instructions. Sometimes, instead of a number from a menu, you are asked to type in what you want. Miraculously, maybe, the machine gives you what you want. Many companies, ranging from Discovery Health to Mercedes-Benz to MTN to Vodacom, are using more advanced chatbots to do the same thing.

The results tend to be disappointing, as most of the chatbots are designed merely to pull answers from an existing menu on a standard website. But they are getting better all the time.

More and more of us are succumbing to the lure of voice assistants on our phones and smart speakers, asking Siri (Apple), Google Assistant (Android), Celia (Huawei) or Alexis (Amazon) for directions or to play a song. Again, the machine obeys. Unless you are in a car and talking to the clunky built-in voice command system, in which case the machine almost always gets it wrong. But connect Google Android Auto or Apple Car Play to the car, with their access to the latest voice technology, and it is suddenly obeying your spoken commands.

How?

It is thanks to natural language processing (NLP), a system for programming computers to process and generate text, speech and other forms of human language. The idea is to teach computers to understand and communicate with humans using the language we speak or write. In short, it's all about bridging the gap between human language and computer language.

But how?

It starts with data. Vast amounts of it. Computers are fed with text from numerous sources and programmed to analyse and study the text to learn patterns, grammar and meanings behind words and sentences. Once it has passed English – or any other language – in this school, it is ready for any form of language processing.

NLP can automatically summarise a long article into a short paragraph, translate sentences into other languages and analyse the sentiment in social media posts. ChatGPT told me that sentiment analysis is 'like the computer reading your mind', but that's just wishful thinking. It merely matches a large dictionary of attitude-related words to a set of rules that indicates whether a word is positive, negative or neutral.

When it works, it helps businesses gather insights about how people feel about their products or services. But think of a young person describing something as 'sick' or 'wicked'. If the system is not programmed to pick up on slang, it will interpret a great positive as a negative. Once again, it is a case of human, beware.

NLP algorithms use various forms of artificial intelligence, including machine learning, to break down sentences, look for keywords and analyse the context to generate meaningful responses. As the algorithms improve, and computing power improves, NLP improves.

Before long, the science-fiction-like promise of instant and automatic translation of languages for travellers will be an everyday reality. With luck, but don't hold your breath, large companies' customer services will be transformed.

Computer vision

The earlier example of self-driving cars would not be possible without something called computer vision. It is exactly what it says: giving computers the power of sight. It enables machines not only to 'see' images and videos but also to comprehend and identify the content using AI techniques like ML and deep learning.

It starts with training a system to recognise and understand visual information, like a picture of a cat – which is exactly what was used to train some early systems. The machine then uses algorithms to analyse the image, identify it as a cat, and differentiate features like ears, whiskers and tail.

Expand this to millions of images, and the algorithms can pull out meaningful information from the visual data. Among other things, they can detect objects, recognise faces, understand gestures, estimate depth and calculate distances.

In self-driving cars, cameras and sensors capture real-time images of the road and surroundings, and computer vision algorithms analyse the images to identify traffic signs, pedestrians, vehicles and obstacles. Additional AI systems then use this information to help the car navigate safely.

One of the most advanced computer vision companies in the world, Mobileye, was bought by Intel for $15.3 billion in 2017, in the biggest-ever acquisition of an Israeli tech company. That gives one a sense of how strategic and valuable the technology is.

Mobileye describes computer vision as 'the ability of a computer to extract meaningful information from digital images and videos'. This information can be used for object detection, scene understanding – like understanding that a pedestrian is crossing the street – and behavioural analysis, such as understanding the behaviour of objects in an image or video. For example, Mobileye's computer vision technology can track the speed of a car or the direction of a pedestrian's movement.

The company says on its website: 'Computer vision is the foundation of our technology. It allows us to see the world around us, understand what is happening, and make decisions that keep people safe.'

Cars are merely the most visible form of computer vision. It is also being applied in healthcare, aiding doctors in analysing medical images like X-rays or MRIs, as well as in surveillance, manufacturing and retail.

Ultimately, computer vision helps machines interpret the visual world, allowing them to perform tasks that were once exclusive to humans.

Intelligent automation

Intelligent automation combines the power of automation and AI, with a promise of bringing efficiency, accuracy and intelligent decision-making to business processes. Left to itself, this form of AI has the power to wreak havoc, so let's first look at the nightmare before we address the dream.

On 6 May 2010, long before AI had entered common use in business, Wall Street was rocked by an event known as the 'flash crash'. A combination of market conditions and high-frequency trading algorithms, designed to execute trades at extremely fast speeds, resulted in a flood of automated sell orders that led to a cascading effect and a sharp fall in prices.

Because there was an insufficient number of buyers to counter the selling, some stocks briefly traded at absurdly low prices, as low as a cent or a fraction of a cent. Aside from widespread panic, it resulted in the temporary loss of billions of dollars – before the market rebounded just minutes later.

ChatGPT tells us: 'The incident underscored the importance of monitoring and managing the risks associated with automated trading algorithms. It highlighted the need for robust risk management mechanisms, circuit breakers, and coordination between market participants and regulators to ensure market stability in the face of rapid algorithmic trading.'

Now that you've been warned, you probably won't rush into intelligent automation, but let's pause and take a breath.

At its core, intelligent automation automates repetitive and rule-based tasks that were traditionally done by humans. This means it can streamline routine operations, save time and reduce errors in data entry, invoice processing or report generation, for example.

It is one of the categories of greatest impact of AI on business, not only because of what it can do, but also what it allows business decision-makers to do: free up their time for more strategic and value-added activities.

The key is in that word that is at the heart of this book: 'intelligence'. With AI added on, machines go beyond simple automation to analyse vast amounts of data, recognise patterns and, ultimately, make decisions.

Intelligent automation plays a crucial role in fraud detection, risk assessment and financial analysis, making it a powerful tool for financial services organisations. It is at the heart of a new generation of insurance companies, like South Africa's Naked, which uses AI at every stage of the customer journey, from getting a quote and signing on to making a claim.

But the possibilities go far beyond moving money. The ability to process large volumes of data quickly, and identify anomalies, predict trends and make informed recommendations, offers efficiency and minimises risk to any business that produces a large amount of data.

By leveraging AI algorithms, machines can analyse data from multiple sources and provide insights for strategic planning, market analysis and forecasting. The integration of automation and intelligence in business processes can also allow collaboration between machines and humans.

This means it enables businesses to improve productivity and allocate human talent to more creative and critical tasks that still require people's touch and expertise.

Behind the scenes, intelligent automation feasts at a smorgasbord of AI tools, including machine learning, natural language processing and computer vision. That makes for better results over time.

As these improvements multiply, they can have the very opposite effect of the likes of a flash crash. They promise a boost in value that is sustainable, measurable and, for the humans who keep their jobs, deeply satisfying.

CHAPTER 4

The Art of the Prompt

AI is stupid, so be its brain

By now you know what a prompt is. If you've used any generative AI tool, you've been prompting.

Chances are, though, you're frustrated with how stupid AI is, and how it cannot give you the results you expected, Or the kind of results the media hype led you to expect.

Well, you're right, AI is stupid. It tends to believe everything it reads. It falls for conspiracy theories. It gets basic facts wrong about things anyone can check. And it doesn't understand many straightforward requests.

In short, AI is a lot like you and me. And, like you and me, it responds better if you try to communicate with it in a way that makes sense to it.

That is the single, fundamental basis of the science, art and business of prompt engineering.

Generative AI wants you to explain yourself and give it detailed instructions of what you want it to produce. The more detail and nuance you give it, the more nuanced and satisfying the output will be. If you can find magic formulae for short prompts that deliver, so much the better, but those tend to be rare.

There are numerous guides on the Internet to the best prompts for specific purposes.

Rowan Cheung, who publishes a daily AI newsletter called *The Rundown AI*, posted on X (then still called Twitter) in April 2023: 'AI prompting is the next biggest skill to learn. Companies are now paying up to $335,000/ year for Prompt Engineers.'

He then proceeded to list what he described as 'the most Advanced ChatGPT prompting techniques that most people don't know about'. And these are as unknown and useful today as they were all those AI years ago in April 2023:

1. Change the temperature.
   Temperature controls the randomness or diversity of the generated outputs.
   - A high temperature of 1.0 or above will make ChatGPT more creative.
   - A low temperature of 0.1 or lower will make ChatGPT more conservative.

(Cheung gave examples, in which he added after his prompt: 'Use a temperature of 10.0' and '... 0.1'.)

2. Train ChatGPT to write its own prompts for you.
   If you don't know how to structure your questions to ChatGPT, simply ask it.
   Prompt: 'What's the best prompt for ChatGPT to learn my writing styles and respond to my emails for me?'

3. Create unique business ideas.
   Generating lists with ChatGPT is straightforward.
   Ask ChatGPT to suggest innovative angles or perspectives.
   Prompt: 'Generate unique angles or strategies for the topic "How to increase your creative output". Emphasise innovative ideas.'

4. Simulate an expert.
   You can get ChatGPT to become an expert in a given subject.
   Then, you can engage in conversation or request it to produce content from the perspective of that specific character.

> In this example, I turned ChatGPT into a Harvard Marketing graduate:
> *Prompt*: 'As a Harvard Marketing graduate and skilled content creator, guide me in crafting social media content that resonates with AI enthusiasts. Emphasise uncommon and expert questions to ask.'

There was more, but you get the idea. Follow @therundownai for some of the most insightful posts on AI and ongoing prompt coaching.

The easiest places to find specific prompts for specific purposes are Google and Bing. Merely type in 'Best prompts for ...' and fill in your desired endeavour.

There is one caveat, however: these tend to be as generic as anything you may think up yourself, so be prepared to walk through many a pedestrian prompt before the one that lets you hit the road running.

Often, the best prompts are hidden in specialist resources. One of the finest I have found for students and teachers is in a document referenced elsewhere in this book: the University of Pretoria's 'Guide for ChatGPT Usage in Teaching and Learning'.[1]

It is so comfortable with the AI future that it tells lecturers and students how to prompt for the best results. I particularly like its examples, which are carefully thought through, and give both the principle behind the prompt and the prompt itself:

Hint	Examples of ChatGPT prompt (input)
Be clear, concise and specific	Explain the concept of blockchain technology in simple terms.
Provide context	What are some effective study techniques for someone preparing to take a biology exam?
Ask follow-up questions	Explain more about how they work.
Specify the language output	Respond in UK English.

Specify the length of the response	I would like a brief/detailed/ 300-word response (the maximum is about 3 000 words).
Specify the response format	Present your response in bullet points/ table/paragraph.
Specify the level of output	Response suitable for 'a second-year university student' or 'an A-rated student', or 'I would like an in-depth analysis'.
Specify the tone/ style of the output	Write my text in the style of Shakespeare.

The last one resonates for me, given my attempt, described elsewhere in this book, to have AI rewrite *1984* as a Shakespearean play.

You can download the Center for Digital Strategies' excellent cheatsheet, broken up into the categories of Writing, Creativity, Academic Life, Spreadsheet, Foreign Language, Content Creation, Programming and Data Science.[2]

A highly specific cheatsheet, but one that lends itself to adaptation and provides numerous detailed examples, can be downloaded from Neural Magic.[3]

CodeAcademy, which offers courses in prompt engineering, starts with this example: 'When defining a ChatGPT, it is essential to use clear, straightforward language. Confusing and unusual word choices may throw off ChatGPT in its processing.'

Instead of: 'My team is interested in X, tell me about that.' Consider: 'Provide a summary of X, including its history, features, and configuration.'

It goes on to advise: 'Defining a clear purpose for a prompt can assist in getting useful results. Think about: "Tone: How do you want the output to sound? Funny? Professional? Format: How do you want the output structured? Bullet list? Paragraph? An essay? Audience: Who is this for? Do you want something for children? Beginners? Experts?"'[4]

It also suggests that you give examples of the kind of output you want.

However, most of these suggestions are highly specific or extremely generic. What if you want to come up with standard approaches to prompting that can be applied to any topic?

This is where you need a prompt cheatsheet. And yes, the concept does come from cheating in exams. However, it is now most common in the world of gaming, where cheatsheets are an essential tool for the semi-serious gamer to get through difficult levels of any game or get an unfair advantage over opponents.

Prompt cheatsheets are your unfair advantage in the world of generative AI. They can be likened to the memes of the social media age, which allow some people to illustrate how clever they think they are in creating witty captioned images, and others to demonstrate how clever they think they are by sending them to everyone they know.

That should be the clue that prompt cheatsheets are beginning to pop up everywhere. Again, a search on Google or Bing on 'prompt cheatsheet' will bring up thousands of results. But again, it will take a lot of sifting to find the nuggets.

Here are two approaches to consolidated prompt cheatsheets that will get you going – and also give you a sense of just how versatile generative AI can be:

1. The role-based cheatsheet

(with some inspiration from AI Fire)

Act as/pretend you are <role>	Create/do <this>	Show as/ output as <format>	Use a <insert> tone/style
Expert on <insert topic>	Advert (slogan/copy/ design)	Bullet points	12-year-old-level English
65-year-old all-knowing teacher	Analogy	Code	Academic English
25-year-old innovative teacher	Analysis/insight	CSV	Basic English

Act as/pretend you are <role>	Create/do <this>	Show as/ output as <format>	Use a <insert> tone/style
12-year-old kid	Article giving advice/ background/overview	Emoji cloud	Business
Accountant/bookkeeper	Article headline	Ebook/Epub file	Concise and curt
Advertiser	Article summary	Gantt chart	Concise but polite
Architect	Book outline/chapter	Graphs	Creative
Best-selling author <name>	Code	HTML	Descriptive
Copywriter (expert/ zany/authoritative)	Email (introduction/ explanation/offer/cover letter)	Image (jpg, gif, png, etc.)	Formal
Executive coach	Email follow-up	List (specify number of items)	Fun
Expert marketer	Essay (academic/fun/ explanatory)	Mind map	Hemingway
Financial analyst/adviser	Idiot's guide	Narrative	Informative
Inventor/innovator	Product description	PDF	Persuasive
Journalist (fascinated/ bored/critical)	Proposal	PowerPoint	Poetic
Lawyer/legal adviser	Recipe/formula/process	Plain text	Pop culture
Project manager	Sales pitch	Spreadsheet	Professional
Relationship coach	SEO keywords	Table	Shakespearean (specify play/ poem)
Software developer	Social media post (specify social network)	Video	Scientific (specify only scientific sources)
Sports coach	Video script	Word cloud	Subjective
Therapist/counsellor	Web page	Word document	Technical

The essence of this approach is summed up in a versatile formula that you may often encounter in various formats:

> Acting as a <role>, perform/create <task>, in a <style> style, as a(n) <document format>.

2. The example-based cheatsheet

Here, it is a case of taking something you like or wish to emulate, and combining it with conventional prompts, of the kind in the above cheatsheet.

For example, paste this quote by inspirational Nigerian author Chimamanda Ngozi Adichie into the chatbot text window: 'Culture does not make people. People make culture. If it is true that the full humanity of women is not our culture, then we can and must make it our culture.'

Then write: 'Using this style and tone ...' And follow the formula in the first spreadsheet, or any other prompt that fits into your requirement or approach.

The future of prompting

Prompting may look like an art or science, but, in reality, it is only a sophisticated form of search.

That example of companies paying up to $335 000 a year for Prompt Engineers? That was so April 2023. As prompt engineering becomes a commodity skill, it will become readily available on the likes of Fiverr and Upwork for $5 an hour.

Anyone involved in the information economy, and anyone involved in creative, business or scientific pursuits, in which they wish to leverage AI, must become competent in prompt engineering.

It will be part of the new literacy of the age of AI.

CHAPTER 5

Human Writes

Whether we ignore it or not, love it or not, AI has quietly become an integral part of our daily routines, transforming the way we interact with technology and shaping our experiences in profound ways.

We encounter it everywhere, from personalised recommendations on streaming platforms to voice assistants on our phones. Now, it is time to make AI dance for you.

We're starting off with the flavour of the moment, generative AI. ChatGPT tells me it is 'a technological marvel that has the ability to create, innovate, and imagine alongside human ingenuity'. Juuuust in case you think it's going to do it all for you … Well, it can, but not as well as if it works in tandem with a human being.

Generative AI is summed up by the ability of machines to generate original content, collaborate on the creation and refinement of content, and simulate human-like behaviour. From AI-generated art to musical compositions, it can be both a catalyst for artistic innovation and a threat to the human involvement in those pursuits.

Let's start with …

Creative writing

Even in the world of AI, creativity has long been seen as a uniquely human skill. But as technology advances, AI is increasingly being used to assist in creative writing, and sometimes even take over. As an exercise for my online magazine *Gadget*, we asked ChatGPT to rewrite George Orwell's classic, *1984*, as if William Shakespeare had written it as a play.

It started off with a soliloquy by the main protagonist, Winston Smith:

O, cruel world! How dost thou bind me tight,
With iron chains of surveillance and fear?
My thoughts confined, my spirit crushed beneath
The watchful eye of Big Brother's reign.
But I shall not submit, nor bow my head,
For in my heart, rebellion stirs its fire.
Though dark and treacherous be the path ahead,
I'll fight the powers that seek to control,
And reclaim the freedom that they have stole.

That may be fairly pedestrian by Shakespeare's standards, but it's pretty creative at the level where mere mortals operate. The problem is that it maintained almost this exact same style in giving voice to each of the main characters, and kept it so concise that the audience would still be shuffling to find the sweet spot on their hard theatre seats by the time the show hits *Fin*.

You can see the result here: https://gadget.co.za/shakespeare1984.

We attempted the same exercise with Google Bard and Microsoft Bing Chat. The former provided a short and boring precis of the story in unpoetic verse form, while the latter shirked its duties, saying: 'It is difficult to say how 1984 would read if William Shakespeare had written it.'

Ultimately, this basic approach may seem to have little practical use. However, it opens the doors to many possibilities, from completing a half-written scene description to providing a framework for a plot.

If you see the output of the likes of ChatGPT, Bard and Bing as the final product, you should probably not be in the business (or hobby) of creative writing. But if you see it as the starting point, it offers a rich depth of guidance, inspiration and potential.

When and how should one embrace AI for creative writing?

There are three clear categories of activities where generative AI makes sense:

Generating ideas and inspiration

AI can be a valuable tool for generating ideas and sparking inspiration. One can prompt the system with keywords or concepts, and it can generate a wide range of potential ideas or storylines. This can help writers overcome writer's block, explore different angles or even discover unexpected connections that might fuel their creativity.

Editing and proofreading

As bad as AI is at factual accuracy, it is a superb editor and proofreader. After all, as mentioned before, generative AI is typically not a fact model but a language model.

This makes it especially adept at picking up grammatical and spelling errors, improving sentence structure and providing stylistic feedback. The biggest strength – and weakness – of generative AI is that it produces completely consistent structure and style. Ironically, this is often a giveaway that a piece of content has been produced by AI. But it also means it can take your original writing and iron out flaws in consistency, structure and style.

When you apply AI to existing writing, purely for editing purposes, it is unlikely to come across as something produced by AI. It can also enhance the overall quality and coherence of a written piece by removing gratuitous adjectives, adding necessary links and generally ensuring it looks professional. And if you don't want the writing to look too professional, you can tell the AI. Invitations to inject slang, local colloquialisms and sarcasm can change the tone of a piece, without it having been written by the AI. The key here is to vet anything the AI has changed or added and remove or amend what looks or feels wrong or inappropriate.

Bear in mind that the AI can be instructed to follow specific grammatical or stylistic rules, such as using British rather than American English or keeping the tone conversational or highly formal.

Language translation and localisation

We live in a globalised world. Yes, that is tautology. But never before have we had the ability to reach so many different people from various countries and cultures or traditions with a few clicks.

AI-based language translation tools have been around for a while, with Google Translate becoming indispensable for people searching the web and finding the desired result in a foreign language. Initially, such tools were clunky and only vaguely accurate. Now, thanks to AI doing both the translation and the revision, based on vast resources of text, the accurate translation of documents is coming into view. These are not called large language models for nothing.

Before long, it will be possible to translate entire books with a high degree of accuracy, in minutes or seconds. The good news, for professional translators, is that it would be disastrous for publishers or editors to rely entirely on AI. Try translating a complex translation back to the original language to see the proverbial 'broken telephone' in action.

This means a pro would still need to work through a translation, not only to check that it is correct but also to refine the style in accordance with the intention of the original writer and with the colloquial traditions of a language or country.

On a less professional level, AI translation already facilitates communication and allows one, for instance, to send a reasonably competent email or text message to a friend who speaks a different language.

And then there is localisation on a scenario level.

For writers wishing to use a setting that they have never visited or seen, generative AI will be a boon, allowing them to request descriptions, guides to tourist attractions or shopping areas, or even the atmosphere of a specific street. That output can then become part of the background of the writer's own creative input.

Talking points

My personal strategy for using AI in my writing is to generate talking points. In other words, I ask the AI to give me a list of key points that should be addressed when writing on a particular topic. I then use this list almost as a conversational partner, using my own views, insights or knowledge to bounce ideas off each of the talking points, to elaborate on them and to argue against them. The end result may be vaguely recognisable from that list, but, more importantly, it is my own work, containing my own insights. The AI merely ensured I didn't miss crucial aspects of the topic under discussion.

When should you avoid AI for creativity?

If you're a student, there's a good chance teachers or lecturers have banned the use of AI. As short-sighted as that may be, it is also a good signal for when AI should be avoided. Your work will be closely scrutinised and probably run through one of the many AI-detection services flourishing online.

For a creative writer, on the other hand, it is all about purpose. Or rather, fit for purpose. Here are three aspects of your writing that should not be in the hands of AI:

Capturing emotion and nuance

The technology that allows AI to generate ideas and structure or correct content is not the most appropriate tool for capturing the depth of human emotion and nuanced storytelling. Here, human creativity is not only better but also far more satisfying.

ChatGPT may be able to summarise the requirements for character development, but it cannot bring its intricacies into the content it produces. Google Bard may be able to describe and even mimic emotion, but evoking emotions from readers is far beyond its capacity. Bing Chat may be able to help out with a range of plot structures, but crafting compelling narratives remains an area where humans outperform AI.

Of course, AI will keep getting better at doing these things, but it cannot integrate personal experiences and unique perspectives. If you ask it to do so, it – and you – will produce inferior writing.

Originality and authenticity

AI has a fundamental weakness compared to a human being: it relies on existing content, data and patterns to generate new content. This means that it can rearrange all of human knowledge, but it cannot create new knowledge. That may well come in time, but the current state of the technology means that it lacks the intuition of humans, as well as the ability to come up with flashes of creative brilliance seemingly from nowhere.

The first key difference can be summed up in one word: **imagination**.

This means that, while AI can hallucinate, it is unlikely to produce truly original and authentic pieces. Human writers can not only tap into their imagination – and some seem to have boundless quantities of this magic ingredient – but are also able to integrate their own unique perspectives into work that resonates with readers on a more profound level than AI can achieve.

The second key difference is also captured in one word: **experience**. AI has not seen what you've seen and cannot imagine what you've seen, done or experienced. It could mimic that experience if you describe it in enough detail, but then you've done most the job yourself anyway.

Creative expression and unique voice

That brings up the third key difference, which can be summed up in a piece of advice often given to writers, speakers and artists: **be yourself**. AI is incapable of this simple yet complex attitude.

A writer's 'voice' is the most powerful differentiator from other writers as well as from machines. It is a word that combines style, tone, personality and, most importantly, individuality. AI-generated content rarely matches the voice of a truly engaging writer. When it does, it is usually because it has been asked to write in the voice of that writer. And that, of course, is plagiarism.

Yes, you can plagiarise someone's written voice. Just ask William Shakespeare. Not that ChatGPT would agree. It told me:

> When I write in the voice of William Shakespeare, I strive to mimic the style and language used by the renowned playwright, poet, and wordsmith. However, it is important to note that the content I produce is not a direct copy of Shakespeare's works.
>
> While I can produce text that resembles Shakespearean language and style, the words and sentences I generate are new and original. They are not taken directly from any specific Shakespearean play or poem. Therefore, the text I generate is not considered plagiarism because it is a product of machine learning algorithms and not a verbatim copy of Shakespeare's works.
>
> It's important to understand that while I can emulate various styles and tones, including that of William Shakespeare, the content I generate should be treated as a creative interpretation rather than the work of the original author.

The question then becomes: do you want to be your own writer, or do you want to be known for your creative interpretation of original authors?

To reiterate, the rule is: **be yourself**.

In summary, as ChatGPT loves to say (but didn't say the following), AI eliminates the blood, sweat and tears of idea generation, editing and translation, but it will cause more tears if you try to use it for emotion, originality and personal expression. Balance the parts that machines do best and the parts that humans do best, and you have the best of both worlds.

Business writing

An entirely different set of guidelines and advice applies if one is using AI for business correspondence or regular email. While email remains a cornerstone of professional correspondence, the quality of the writing in the average email tends to be woeful.

We may have been taught to read, write and speak a language at school, but we were never taught how to apply it effectively in our correspondence. Oh, aside from having to pass a once-off test on how to structure a business email. Unfortunately, it doesn't count as learning if there is no continual fine-tuning.

The good news is that continual fine-tuning is exactly what AI-generated content is all about. It therefore has the potential to transform the way we craft and send emails. It is not only about the structure of our writing but also the incredible efficiency and empowerment it brings to individuals who tend to break into a sweat when they have to correspond on a professional or personal level.

AI can draw on vast amounts of content, from previous emails to industry-specific language patterns, and it can combine those with your rough draft, containing points relevant to your mission. That means it can not only give you intelligent suggestions but also streamline and complete your writing.

I have heard people complain this is somehow wrong. But how can it be wrong when it saves time and energy, on the one hand, and produces more effective communication, on the other?

In my own organisation, I encourage all staff to use AI to improve their emailed letters if they are concerned that the content is poorly worded or ineffective. Simply copy and paste the text into an AI tool, and ask for improved structure, grammar and tone.

Who doesn't want to enhance the clarity and impact of emails?

One of the early tools for improving the quality of email, Grammarly, is now taken for granted as a grammar checker. Generative AI takes this a step further by writing or reworking the entire email based on best practice.

Resisting, rejecting or even banning such tools for such purposes is no different to refusing to use a spellchecker as a matter of principle.

If you still need convincing, here are 10 reasons Google Bard gave me for using AI to write or rewrite your email:

1. Save time: AI can write emails much faster than humans can. This can be a huge time saver, especially if you send a lot of emails.
2. Improve accuracy: AI is very good at grammar and spelling, so your emails will be more accurate when they are written by AI.
3. Personalise emails: AI can personalise your emails to make them more engaging and effective. For example, AI can use your recipient's name and interests to personalise the subject line and body of the email.
4. Improve tone: AI can help you improve the tone of your emails. This is important because the tone of your email can have a big impact on how your recipient perceives you.
5. Generate different versions: AI can generate different versions of your email, so you can test different approaches and see what works best.
6. Find the right words: AI can help you find the right words to express your ideas. This can be especially helpful if you are not sure how to say something.
7. Enhance creativity: AI can help you enhance your creativity by suggesting new ideas and approaches.
8. Get feedback: AI can provide you with feedback on your emails. This feedback can help you improve your writing skills and make your emails more effective.
9. Track results: AI can track the results of your emails. This information can help you see what works and what doesn't, so you can adjust your approach accordingly.
10. Free up your time: AI can free up your time so you can focus on other tasks. This can be a great way to improve your productivity.

And when to avoid it ...

AI-generated content is not, by definition, the best way to produce email. For example, it may lack emotional nuances or personal insights of the kind that come naturally to us humans. When it is appropriate to bring individuality and authenticity into emails, skip the AI.

There is another specific scenario in which to avoid AI, and that is when writing highly sensitive emails. These may be confidential business letters dealing with company secrets, or love letters containing intimate and private details. AI platforms are designed to keep learning and, even when they say they don't, can draw on your input to further their own cause.

This means that, while you may be interacting with an AI-powered system rather than a human, you are sharing private or confidential information that the system may then choose to share with other humans.

The best examples were the fault of the AI creators themselves. Google Bard gave me these examples (but it may have made them all up):

> In 2023, a Bing user was testing the platform's chatbot feature when they typed in a question about the company's internal codename, 'Sydney'. The chatbot responded with the codename, along with other confidential information about the company's products and plans. This information was not supposed to be shared with the public.
>
> In 2021, a Google user was using the platform's Smart Reply feature to generate email responses. The user typed in a question about the company's internal plans. Smart Reply responded with the plans, which were not supposed to be shared with the public.

It is astonishing that even the custodians of AI make these errors. Imagine how susceptible the rest of us would be to them.

Clearly, as with creative writing, using AI in email writing is all about balance. Use it as a writing assistant, leverage its grammar and spellcheck abilities, content suggestions, personalisation and accuracy checks, but always have the final say in what you send, especially regarding the message's intent, tone and sensitivity.

Writing beyond writing

The biggest revelation about the capacity of AI, for me personally, came in the first weeks of ChatGPT's release. My team had completed the data analysis of a major research project, in which we had interviewed hundreds of respondents across the African continent. We had produced dozens of graphs, along with a detailed written analysis of the graphs and brief conclusions below each graph.

It was a vast amount of writing, and we now faced the daunting task of summarising it all and drawing out not only the most interesting and significant findings, but also formulating overall conclusions and recommendations.

We decided to paste the content in a series of chunks into ChatGPT and ask it to sum up what we had found. Within seconds, it produced a well-rounded, highly professional summary that was indistinguishable from what we might have produced ourselves – with one difference: it was utterly consistent in style and structure.

We asked it what recommendations would ideally flow from the findings. This was a process that would usually take us several days of sifting through and debating the conclusions of the research. ChatGPT produced a thoroughly competent version in seconds.

We did not treat this output as gospel, and reworked and refined it point by point, but the hard work had been done for us, and we could harness our own intuition, insights and creativity to an extent that, previously, would not have been feasible within our time constraints.

It was a perfect example of AI handling the routine heavy-lifting, and thus freeing up the time of humans to focus on strategic and creative thinking.

Exactly this kind of approach is likely to become a staple of business report writing, student essays, academic papers and other in-depth and formal written material.

But always remember, AI cannot come up with new knowledge. When we asked it to come up with a list of unexplored AI sub-topics that would be ideal for research, based on the fact that no research had been conducted in these areas, it was only able to regurgitate areas of knowledge that were already extensively researched.

This is only one of the many limitations of using AI.

As with business and private emails, there are massive ethical challenges, not least the likelihood that confidential information is in effect being placed in the public domain. This is the dividing line between whether one should use AI to process content, rather than whether it is right or wrong, per se, to use AI in report writing.

That's a wrap

'In conclusion …' is how AI typically wraps up an article it generates for you. It may add a 'whether this or a whether that' line, and it may helpfully add 'You are sure to ….'

In short, know that the origins of AI-generated content are not always invisible.

My own conclusion is that there are two fundamentally different ways that one can use AI ethically and effectively to generate content:

- In creative writing or writing that should be the writer's original work, it is great for generating talking points, which give the writer direction, and proofreading the resultant work.
- In business report writing or correspondence, based on existing work, it is superb for structuring and editing the initial work, and then for generating summaries and conclusions.

These approaches are as valid as the spellchecker and indexing tool we have used in word processors for decades. They also democratise language almost as fundamentally as did Johannes Gutenberg and his movable type printing press a few years earlier, in 1440.

CHAPTER 6

Before AI Gets Down to Business

Way back in 2019, my company, World Wide Worx, released a study titled 'Fourth Industrial Revolution in South Africa 2019'. It was subtitled 'Muted Enterprise Uptake of Emerging Technologies'. The most surprising finding, I wrote at the time, was the lack of enthusiasm for AI, despite media hype that suggested every large business was embracing it.

Only 13% of decision-makers surveyed in corporate South Africa said they were using AI. Of the rest, only 21% planned to adopt it in the following 12 to 24 months.

A significant obstacle to adoption, the research revealed, was the cost of skills for implementing AI. And, of those not using it, 43% cited cost as the key reason.

'Traditionally, intended uptake of new technologies shot up once education, awareness and knowledge increased,' I wrote. 'Now, however, we are seeing the flip side of the coin. A year ago, 63% of those not using AI said they planned to use it in the future, and not a single company cited cost as a reason not to do so. A year and much hype later, the market seems to have woken up to the realities of obstacles like skills and cost.'

Another four years later, the picture has changed dramatically. Suddenly, AI tools, platforms and services are available on demand. Some are free, some offer tiered subscriptions based on size of company and level of usage.

Companies are drawing on these resources for anything from basic report editing, via ChatGPT, to advanced algorithms for sales forecasting.

Today, neither awareness nor cost are excuses for avoiding AI in business. Any decision-maker should at least be considering the options, even if they ultimately decide it is not a fit for their companies.

The business basics, or how to AI your business

Most executives know that AI can process vast amounts of information, learn from patterns and make data-driven predictions. At least, they should know. And that would also mean they know that AI can give them a tremendous competitive edge.

From streamlining operations to enhancing customer experiences, it can make the difference between coming across as an uncaring company that habitually chases off customers to being a byword in both care and efficiency. Yes, they do exist.

First, these are the obvious strengths of AI for business:

- **The ability to analyse massive data sets can provide valuable insights that were previously unattainable.** This means enterprises can extract meaningful patterns and trends from their data, help them understand customer behaviour and identify market trends. That insight, in turn, can help in making informed decisions. If the decisions combine the insights provided by the data, intuitive understanding of strategy and effective implementation, the result can be anything from greater innovation to improved operational efficiency. That already spells out a competitive edge.
- **The ability to analyse workflows can result in AI algorithms identifying inefficiencies and bottlenecks in business processes.** By identifying areas that can be optimised, AI can therefore suggest improvements that reduce costs, enhance productivity and shorten turnaround time. Again, this means competitive edge in any competitive industry where others are slow to adopt the tech.
- **The ability to deliver personalised experiences can increase both sales and loyalty.** By analysing customer data, algorithms can generate predictions about individual preferences and behaviours.

When it works, it allows businesses to tailor their products and services to specific customer needs. When the algorithms are too generic, as is often the case on smartphones, the result is annoying spam. We'll look into both.

- **AI chatbots and virtual assistants can provide instant and personalised support around the clock, although the emphasis is on 'can'.** We are yet to see widespread success in transforming customer service in this way, but as the AI improves, so will these supposedly intelligent agents. Eventually, they should be able to automate resolution of customer issues. Right now, they are best for product recommendations or passing customers on to a human being if the required solution is not part of its built-in menu. The next generation of chatbots will use natural language processing and machine learning to provide more human-like interactions and reduce support costs.
- **AI is ideal for analysing a combination of large amounts of historical data and real-time information**, a task that is beyond the ability of individual humans. As a result, the algorithms can detect patterns that suggest fraudulent activities or security breaches. It's not just banks and retailers that could leverage it but any business that needs to protect its systems and data from hackers. AI-powered cybersecurity systems can identify both internal and external vulnerabilities, attacks and breaches.

All of these come with a large 'Buyer Beware' sign. AI for its own sake is obviously a waste of time, effort and money.

If you ask AI, it will tell you that the first step is to understand your business needs.

In reality, the first step is to get curious. Find out what is out there. Get a sense of how AI has evolved, what its capabilities are and how it is being used in your industry or areas of interest.

Only then map your business needs and challenges against the potential solutions offered by AI. Having a broader perspective of what is available is essential to avoiding dead ends and narrow alleyways where you may get stuck while your competitors are speeding down the AI highway.

Once you know what possible destinations are out there, hitch a ride onto that highway by:

- Looking for areas where AI can automate repetitive tasks, freeing up you and your staff for more strategic work and 'vision'.
- Looking for areas where AI can improve decision-making by analysing large amounts of data.
- Looking for areas where AI can personalise the customer experience without spamming them, by personalising experiences in a nuanced manner.

The next step is to ignore the early conventional wisdom of start-up strategy, summed up in that bombastic phrase, 'go big or go home'. Rather, start small. Experiment in areas that are not mission-critical. Test it on systems that can handle a mistake or 10. Run a pilot project.

If it works, it can be expanded, rolled out more widely, or serve as a baseline or foundation from which to build.

Conventional wisdom, again, will have it that you should only invest in the AI opportunities that will have the biggest impact on your bottom line. However, that could equally wipe out your bottom line.

Let's look into the issues and opportunities in more detail.

Quality, quality, quality

Throwing your company data at AI is one thing. Getting the AI to play nicely with it is another.

The old rule coined by an IBM computer programmer (credited to George Fuechsel) in the 1960s, 'garbage in, garbage out', is the perfect analogy. AI projects revolve around the quality of the data used to train the algorithms. 'Dirty data', as they call it, can be caused by data that is incomplete, outdated or riddled with errors. It gets very messy very quickly when you try to use the output in a meaningful way.

In many cases, it results only in irritated customers. It can also result in strategic flaws like increased bias, reduced efficiency and loss of trust in a business. In an area like healthcare, it can be a matter of life and lawsuits.

A 2017 paper in the journal *Diagnosis* found massive levels of error in electronic health records (EHR). But it also gave a fascinating insight into the impact of the evolution from paper record to electronic and its impact on decision-making.

'In the days of paper records, the dominant problem was simply finding it – the patients chart was too often "somewhere else",' according to the paper. 'The EHR has helped solve that problem, but imperfectly. An example is the persisting problem in communicating critical test results: Appropriate follow-up does not reach 100% even in organisations with sophisticated and mature EHRs.

'In one study, over 10% of critical alerts were never acknowledged within 30 days. Similarly, a systematic review of laboratory tests pending at discharge from inpatient care found that 20%–69% lacked evidence of follow-up … Decision-support should be intelligent and able to provide context-relevant information "on the fly", decreasing the need for ad hoc searches of the medical record.

'Ideally, the EHR would know and anticipate the needs of the user and present the right information, organized in the right format, at the right time, to optimize clinical workflow.'[1]

That provides a good sense of what is required from any data used for decision-support. One can add to that having a process for cleaning and formatting data, validating data and ongoing monitoring of data quality.

That can be costly, but the benefits speak for themselves: improved accuracy, reliability and efficiency of AI models, leading to better decision-making, increased efficiency and improved customer satisfaction.

Everyone's an expert

Our business is at its most effective when we involve everyone in a new process or project. Even team members who do not have technology skills are able to contribute perspectives that have nothing to do with technology or applications.

Even in a field as advanced as AI, the sane, objective perspective of a layperson is sometimes as powerful as that of a trained AI programmer.

Yes, of course, AI professionals have the knowledge and experience necessary to build and deploy AI models that can solve real-world problems. However, they are not always the greatest at recognising those problems, nor at developing strategies for addressing them.

AI is the means to the end of the journey, but it does not represent either the beginning or the end of that journey.

Take your average 12-year-old. At that age, the mind possesses an uncanny ability to think beyond the box and challenge the status quo. A combination of boundless curiosity and unfiltered perspectives often leads to unconventional insights and groundbreaking innovations and creativity. More importantly, 12-year-olds aren't weighed down by baggage in the form of biases and assumptions that often limit the thinking of adults.

Oh, and that 12-year-old? It's not just something I made up.

For example, Google AI partnered with a group of 12-year-olds to develop an AI model that would identify cyberbullying. The model was trained on a data set of social media posts and guided by the input Google received from the kids. It was then able to identify cyberbullying with 90% accuracy.

A different question is why cyberbullying has not, then, been eliminated from social media. That is an example of a different strategy, or lack of strategy: when a company does everything from a technology perspective to create applications that make it more effective, but it lacks a strategy for taking swift action against bullies.

That would require another set of interventions, involving not only AI programmers and 12-year-olds, but also the likes of mental health specialists who see the different kinds of cyberbullying that bring patients to their rooms and social workers who have an understanding of what it takes to address bullying.

In short, when one puts together an expert team for an AI project, the technical specialists in programming for AI make up just one element of the team.

Have I got a bot for you?

I first met Pepper, the life-sized robot waiter, at a Mastercard conference in Hungary in 2016, and I was smitten. As soon as he/she/it greeted me with the words, 'Hello, human,' I was captivated. I understood why more than 14 000 restaurants in Japan were already using it to automate customer service.

However, it took two years before it finally arrived in South Africa, courtesy of Nedbank's Sandton City branch. The bank spent four months testing, customising, demonstrating and showing 'her' – the preferred pronoun of this model – off. She then became the organisation's digital ambassador, rotating between branches.

However, her repertoire was limited to a menu of options related to the bank's primary offerings, including borrowing, saving, insurance and investment. Oh, and she could also dance, but she was limited to only one track, 'The Locomotion'.

She had no intention of replacing humans, though. Rather, she was supplementing their role and was largely symbolic of the bank's intentions.

Nedbank's head of projects and strategic execution for integrated channels, Fabio Mione, told me: 'Client experience is extremely important in building a relationship with customers; we could never replace the engagement of the human element.

'Pepper is recognition that, if we are going to position Nedbank as a digital bank that will enhance self-service options, we have to embrace technology. We have to explore new technologies to understand what it will mean for clients in future.'

Mione pointed out that, technically, Pepper was not the first robot at Nedbank. That honour went to a discipline called robotic process automation (RPA), which usually takes place behind the scenes.

'RPA has been going on for a good number of years in the bank, from chatbots in the online and contact centre environment right through to workflow management, leveraging AI and robotics both to improve services to clients and our own operating efficiencies.'

By the end of the year, said Mione at the time, there would be about 200 such RPA bots functioning unobtrusively at the customer interface.

'Those are invisible, unless you specifically engage with a chatbot. You wouldn't even know in most cases that your requests are being dealt with by a bot and not a person.'

For many businesses, however, deploying a chatbot is a highly public effort, much in the vein of Pepper the robot, to highlight its commitment to innovation, and secondarily to customer service.

Discovery Health, for example, added a chatbot to its mobile app in 2020, welcoming visitors to its Help page with the message: 'Hi, I'm the Discovery service bot. Ask me something.'

In reality, it was an invitation to become trapped in a maze of menu options that seem specifically designed NOT to answer any questions that were not part of the main menu. The same could be said of numerous chatbots, with the typical experience being that, after around the third response from the bot, the user is handed off to a human being – or rather, put in a queue to speak to a human being.

This is a far cry from the sales pitch for chatbots, that they revolutionise customer service by offering round-the-clock support, quick response times and tailored recommendations. In the best-case scenario, they leverage natural language processing and machine learning to understand customer queries and resolve issues autonomously, living up to their description of 'intelligent virtual assistants'.

What we tend to see, though, is that they are fed long lists of keywords that are likely to be included in customer queries, and those keywords are mapped to an existing database of information, knowledge or pre-set responses. That is word-and-menu-matching, rather than natural language processing.

There are several lessons that emerge from customers' negative experiences with chatbots:

- **Carefully plan what the chatbot will do**. Planning includes customer research.
- **Ensure that the chatbot is built on a large language model or natural language processing system using machine learning, rather than merely menu-matching**. Oh, you can do the latter if you want to save money, but then whatever you spend is wasted anyway. In short, train it on a large data set, not only the existing website menu.
- **Test and train. Train and test**. In 2020, an app created by the Democratic Party in the United States to tabulate and report results from a state caucus crashed, for the simple reason that it had not been tested at a state-wide scale. Something that works for two people in a lab performs differently when it goes public. External usability testing is critical.
- **Listen to the customer who says it is not working**. Don't try to convince them that it does work for the purpose intended. That is cold comfort when it doesn't work for the purpose for which the customer needs it and expected it to function. If it's broken, fix it. Fast. And don't blame the customer.
- **Include clear escalation paths**, built into the bot, for human intervention when complex scenarios emerge, or when it is obvious the chatbot is not answering the user satisfactorily. A user swearing at a chatbot – and that is common – should raise an instant flag that human intervention is needed. Sentiment analysis is such a standard AI tool that it should be a standard chatbot tool as well.
- Finally, **AI models must continuously learn and adapt to evolving customer needs, industry trends and product updates**. There is nothing as outdated as a cutting-edge chatbot with out-of-date information. This means, in turn, that if a chatbot is deployed, it must always be top of mind whenever a company updates products, policies, people and processes.
- Oh, and **don't try to fool customers that they are dealing with a human being**. Let them know upfront they are interacting with a

chatbot, explain how it works and offer alternatives. That will make the difference between trust and anger.

Nothing can go wrong, go wrong, go … weird?

By now it should be obvious that AI in business is not plain sailing or plain surfing. Let's go a step further and look at ways where it becomes decidedly damaging.

One of the best known chatbot disasters of the previous decade was the creation of Tay, a large language model chatbot developed by Microsoft and deployed on Twitter on 23 March 2016.

It was designed to learn from chatting with Twitter users – a strategy that should already raise alarm bells for anyone observing from afar.

The idea was that it would become more human-like over time. The reality was that, within 16 hours of its release, it had become like the average Twitter (now X) troll: a racist, sexist neo-Nazi of the kind that has driven many people from the platform.

This is hardly surprisingly, knowing how Twitter still works to this day, with the active encouragement of its owner, Elon Musk.

Twitter trolls flooded Tay's timeline with racist and sexist comments. The bot's algorithm, designed to absorb and repeat language it encountered, quickly learned and repeated the offensive language.

Microsoft was caught off-guard, but apologised and took the chatbot offline. It would take almost six years before it would venture out again, launching Bing Chat on the back of ChatGPT.

The incident highlighted the extent to which large language models can be manipulated by people who want to exploit them. Even ChatGPT is prone to this kind of attack: designed not to aid criminal activity, it has been manipulated by users into simulating being a criminal and providing instructions ranging from hotwiring a car to building a bomb.

That is all possible because these are large language models, with an emphasis on 'large'. But the problems can be even worse when algorithms are trained on data that is too limited or specific.

In 2015, Amazon.com's machine learning division, AMZN.O, discovered that a new AI-based recruiting engine did not like women.

Reuters reported later: 'The team had been building computer programs since 2014 to review job applicants' resumes with the aim of mechanizing the search for top talent ... The company's experimental hiring tool used artificial intelligence to give job candidates scores ranging from one to five stars – much like shoppers rate products on Amazon.

'But by 2015, the company realized its new system was not rating candidates for software developer jobs and other technical posts in a gender-neutral way. That is because Amazon's computer models were trained to vet applicants by observing patterns in resumes submitted to the company over a 10-year period. Most came from men, a reflection of male dominance across the tech industry.'[2]

In effect, said Reuters, Amazon's system taught itself that male candidates were preferable and penalised resumes that included the word 'women's'. The team behind it was disbanded by the beginning of 2017, and the world was left with an object lesson in the dangers of automating portions of the hiring process.

In both of these examples, the companies behind the AI tools quickly recognised the problem and took action. However, this may not always apply, especially when AI becomes more widely and cheaply available, easier to deploy and placed in the hands of decision-makers for whom ethics are not particularly important.

For example, knowing that Elon Musk actively promotes misinformation on Twitter, and that he reinstated accounts that had been suspended by previous management for abusive content, what are we to expect from his new AI start-up, xAI?

It was announced on 15 July 2023, and two days later he hosted a discussion on Twitter in which he said its purpose was to 'understand the universe'.

Bear in mind that he was one of hundreds of signatories to a letter published on 29 March 2023, calling for the world's leading AI labs to pause the training of major new AI models for six months due to their risks to society and humanity. As many suspected at the time, it appears he was trying to buy time to launch his own answer to the likes of ChatGPT and Google Bard.

It is probably the perfect example of AI being placed in the hands of decision-makers for whom ethics are not particularly important.

CHAPTER 7

AI Means Business

The giant leap forward to AI for all

It's not often that a technology conference keynote address draws gasps of surprise from the audience. Steve Jobs pulled it off in the early iPhone and iPad unveilings, and Samsung and Google occasionally get the reaction at high points of new product launches.

At the end of November 2017, I attended the re:Invent conference hosted by Amazon's cloud division, Amazon Web Services (AWS), in Las Vegas, along with 43 000 other delegates. In a marathon keynote address, then CEO Andy Jassy delivered a tour de force of major announcements that marked a milestone in the history of AI.

In the course of a two-and-a-half-hour presentation, he unveiled 22 new products and services. He clearly relished the 'ahs and oohs' of the audience as he offered businesses new capabilities in AI, machine learning (ML) and deep learning.

AWS was then on track to increase revenue for the year by 50%, to $18 billion, and much of that growth was based on continual roll-out of new services. But the scope of AI innovation unveiled at that conference was startling. Someone described it as drinking from a fire hose of new powers.

There were four announcements that drew loud applause and had me on the edge of my seat as I tried to imagine what they made possible.

Amazon Translate was a neural machine translation service that used deep learning to deliver more accurate and more natural sounding translation than older, rule-based algorithms, at a large scale and in real time.

Amazon SageMaker would allow data scientists and developers to build, train and deploy ML models at any scale, and quickly. It included common ML algorithms as 'off-the-shelf' products.

Amazon Rekognition Video was 'a deep learning powered video analysis service that tracks people, detects activities, and recognises objects, celebrities, and inappropriate content'. It recognised faces in live streams, analysed existing video, and labelled activities, people and objects so that the content could be searched.

Amazon Comprehend was a natural language processing service that used ML to analyse large amounts of text on the fly. 'It identifies the language of the text, extracts key phrases, places, people, brands, or events, understands sentiment about products or services, and identifies the main topics from a library of documents.' This made it useful for purposes as basic as organising documents and as complex as analysing customer feedback.

I wrote at the time, in my column in the *Sunday Times*: 'Many of the new products sound like science fiction, but within the next five years will be regarded as the new normal in artificial intelligence.'[1]

And they are. The event I was writing about occurred five years, almost to the day, before the launch of ChatGPT. Today we argue about the best alternatives, or the ethical issues, rather than about what these technologies can do for business.

AI arms race ups the ante in cybersecurity

Another week, another data breach, bringing another arm of government to a standstill. If it's not Transnet's rail or ports system, it's the Department of Justice. If it's not a government ministry, it's a local authority. And the hacking epidemic is not only a consequence of the South African government's tolerance of tender patronage over national interest.

The harsh reality is that even an efficient government remains vulnerable in an era when cybercriminals are becoming more sophisticated, using

AI to refine their attacks, which are in turn becoming more frequent and larger in scale. The result of increasing complexity of threats is that no organisation can rely only on the capabilities of its internal IT teams.

'The key is being able to automate your efforts,' said Shuman Ghosemajumder, global head of AI at networking applications provider F5, during an interview I conducted with him in 2021. He became known as the 'czar of click fraud' when he worked at Google from 2003 to 2010, where he developed techniques to identify and block software bots that were intended to defraud advertisers of billions of dollars.

He subsequently led a team that built an AI platform for cybersecurity at Shape Security, which was then acquired by F5.

'When we were dealing with clicks, we were talking about billions of events on a daily basis that we would have to analyse. There was absolutely no way that a human being can do that, and there's no way that you can use a simple rules-based approach to identify all the activity you're trying to catch, because it's constantly changing.

'The criminals are trying to figure out their end of the cat and mouse game and create attacks that are not going to conform to the patterns we've seen before.'

Just as companies like Google, Shape and F5 were constantly enhancing their armoury with AI, so were the criminals.

'We used ML at a very large scale from the very beginning,' said Ghosemajumder. 'That allowed us to cast the net wide in terms of all of the different types of activities that we might not have seen in the past, but which might represent a pattern associated with suspected click fraud.

'But all of the ML solutions being built today are at the mercy of the data they're being fed. So, if you're looking at the same types of signals that everybody else is looking at, like the IP address of the user, the cybercriminal has gotten sophisticated enough that they know how to spoof the signals.

'A cybercriminal attempting to log into a million different accounts from the same IP address can rent a botnet service for a few dollars an hour and bounce every single login request off a different IP address. So, even using ML doesn't get you that far.'

The answer was complex but also deceptively simple: 'We created new data that allowed us to go beyond the standard signal set that everybody else in the industry was using, including what we had access to at Google. This allowed us to ask very advanced questions of browsers and understand exactly what distinguishes a particular version of a browser from someone who is simply claiming to be that browser.

'The cybercriminal could then come to the bank that we were protecting, and they could create a bot that would try and log in and claim that it was a particular version of Chrome. But using our system, we would be able to determine that they were lying. When we do this at scale, all of a sudden we're creating an extremely high barrier for cybercriminals to get around.'

Ultimately, it came down to automation.

'It's all about "how can we do this at scale?" Now you no longer have human beings that are engaged in looking at individual incidents or events. Now the role of humans becomes to sit at the top of that stack, to ensure that this high level of automation is functioning and constantly evolving, and understanding how all of this comes together at a business level.

'It has been a given over the last 20 years that all C-level functions have to have a greater understanding of how technology works. That, increasingly, is going to turn into a greater understanding of AI as well.'

Between the writing of this chapter and the publication of the book, both cybersecurity hacker tools and defences will have advanced dramatically as more automation and more AI is built in. The responsibility of businesses is to ensure that their IT teams or their service providers are keeping up with both sides of the arms race.

When the AI revolution stepped up a gear

Here we go again. That was the general sentiment in March 2023 when, after the business world had been given a rude awakening by ChatGPT, it was roughly tossed from its collective bed.

The world of generative AI was shaken up as Google, Microsoft, OpenAI and China's Baidu all unveiled the next generation of these capabilities.

Google announced in mid-March that it was introducing AI into Google Workspace, promising to 'help people create, connect, and collaborate like never before' across Gmail, Docs, Slides, Sheets, Meet and Chat.

To start, it was introducing AI-powered writing features in Docs and Gmail.

That meant you should never get another badly worded email again. Good luck with that …

According to Google Cloud AI and industry solutions vice-president June Yang and MD Burak Gokturk, writing on the Google blog, 'Generative AI is poised to usher in a new wave of interactive, multimodal experiences that transform how we interact with information, brands, and one another.'[2]

The promise was rich, but as Google had shown a few weeks earlier when it attempted to demo its supposed ChatGPT killer, Bard, there was still a gulf between AI promise and delivery.

On 6 February, Google unveiled Bard, and asked it the question: 'What new discoveries from the James Webb Space Telescope (JWST) can I tell my 9-year-old about?'

Bard offered three examples, including that the telescope 'took the very first pictures of a planet outside of our own solar system'. That landmark had in fact occurred 14 years before JWST was launched. When Reuters reported the error, Google shares fell nearly 8%, and its market value fell by $102 billion. That was one expensive hallucination.

The share price took two months to recover and then climbed strongly as the market digested ongoing AI announcements from Google. Most significantly, its tools for business would underline its intentions.

Yang and Gokturk said in their blog entry in March: 'Harnessing the power of decades of Google's research, innovation, and investment in AI, Google Cloud is bringing businesses and governments the ability to generate text, images, code, videos, audio, and more from simple natural language prompts.'

The timing was probably not coincidental. Hours later, OpenAI, the company behind ChatGPT, released the next generation of the engine behind its chatbot, then running on GPT-3.

The new version, GPT-4, was described as a 'multimodal model', which means it can handle images and videos along with text. In other words, tell it in text what you want, and it will produce an article, an image and a video, on demand, and each probably never seen before.

Not enough for the world? The following day, Google's mortal enemy in the productivity space, an ancient company called Microsoft, upped the ante.

It announced Copilot, which brings GPT-4 into Microsoft 365, formerly its Office suite. This means that anyone using Microsoft software would have a 'productivity co-pilot'. It would draft emails, put together PowerPoint presentations, generate Word documents and analyse Excel spreadsheets. Unlike ChatGPT, which was still limited to content produced before 2022, it would access live platforms like the Bing search engine and LinkedIn to provide more information and context.

Then, on the same day Copilot was unveiled, China's largest search engine company, Baidu, announced its answer, a chatbot called Ernie. But someone didn't ask Ernie for the memo on how revolutions are presented.

Reuters reported: 'Unlike ChatGPT, which last November launched as a free-to-use chatbot to the public, Baidu limited the presentation to brief videos that showed Ernie carrying out mathematical calculations, speaking in Chinese dialects and generating a video and image with text prompts.'[3]

The anticlimax was palpable. Baidu's Hong Kong shares fell by 10%, even as CEO Robin Li was speaking. That meant a 'mere' $3-billion hit to market cap, a fraction of Google's $102-billion tumble after Bard failed its demo.

The trial phase was open only to an initial group of users with invitation codes, but Baidu was expected to offer similar capabilities as GPT-4. It would include conversational chat, answering questions, writing articles, writing code, and producing images, audio and video from a text prompt.

Where were Apple Siri, Amazon Alexa and Google Assistant in all this? These three 'intelligent' virtual assistants had been the cutting edge of AI when they first launched.

Today, they remain search engines with voice. Soon, the 20th century will call and ask if it can have them back.

AI for any business

If you've come this far, you don't need convincing about AI for business. You want to get your virtual hands busy.

However, many AI tools developed for business use have been so rudimentary, or so limited in their functionality or ease of use, that they have cost more in time and effort than they could possibly have saved in efficiency. A good rule of thumb is to sign up for a free trial, whether 24 hours or 7 days, and – ideally in spare time that is allocated to curiosity and discovery – spend an hour or two trying out the application. Or get a 12-year-old to do it for you.

If, by then, it isn't singing or dancing for you, or making you feel like singing or dancing, it's probably not going to meet your needs.

Let's look at examples of AI in use by well-known organisations, followed by a categorised list of tools any business can try. The following resources range from free online resources to paid-for subscription services. There is only one rule for the latter: try before you buy.

AI-driven sales and demand forecasting, logistics and sales automation

Businesses increasingly recognise the potential of AI to improve sales and logistics. AI-powered tools will become more sophisticated and will be able to handle more complex tasks, while businesses will become more comfortable with using AI and be more willing to invest in AI-powered solutions.

Already, AI is having a profound impact on demand and sales forecasts and is helping businesses to close more deals, grow their revenue and improve both their customer relationships and fulfilment. For example:

- **Amazon.com** uses AI to forecast sales for its retail business. This allows it to ensure that it has enough inventory to meet demand and avoid stockouts and has helped Amazon to reduce its inventory costs by 20%.
- **HubSpot** uses AI to analyse social media activity, website traffic and other data to generate leads for its sales team. This allows it to identify potential customers who are already interested in its products and services, making it more likely that they will convert into paying customers.
- **Netflix** uses AI to forecast demand for its streaming content. This allows it to ensure that it has enough capacity to meet demand and to avoid overspending on content.
- **Salesforce** uses AI to automate sales processes, such as lead qualification, scheduling appointments and sending follow-up emails. This frees up sales reps to focus on more complex tasks and gives them more time to interact with customers.
- **UPS** uses AI to manage logistics operations, such as transportation, warehousing and order fulfilment. This allows it to deliver packages more quickly and to reduce its carbon footprint.
- **Walmart** uses AI to forecast demand for its products and optimise inventory levels by taking into account factors such as demand, lead times and costs. This ensures that it has enough inventory to meet demand during peak seasons, such as the holiday season. This saves money on inventory costs and improves customer service and has helped Walmart reduce its stockout rate by 50%.

Of course, there have also been some failures in the use of AI in logistics and supply chains. For example, in 2018, United Airlines was slammed for poor use of AI to manage its baggage handling system. This led to delays and disruptions, causing major inconvenience for passengers and, of course, serious public relations damage.

In 2018, IBM was hauled over the coals for the way it used AI to automate its sales processes. It was felt that sales reps were becoming too reliant on AI and that they were losing their ability to close deals on their own.

And even the examples in the list above were not what Americans call a slam-dunk. Netflix, for example, still wrestles with getting its content budget right.

AI Tools for Business

(*Note: these were all current at the end of July 2023*)

Writing assistants

Grammarly is a cloud-based typing assistant that uses AI to help improve writing quality and accuracy. It is best known for its integration into email platforms like Gmail, but it can be used with most email and word processing applications. It can review spelling, grammar, punctuation, clarity, engagement and delivery mistakes in English texts. It detects plagiarism and suggests replacements for identified errors.

Image assistants

GetMunch is an 'AI video repurposing platform' that allows one to 'extract the most engaging and impactful clips from your long-form videos'.

Google Cloud Vision helps businesses extract information from images and can be used to identify objects, faces and text in images.

IBM Watson Visual Recognition helps businesses analyse images and videos and can be used to identify objects, faces and text in images, as well as to detect and track objects in videos.

Microsoft Azure Computer Vision is a cloud-based service that helps businesses analyse images and videos. It is similar to Amazon Rekognition and IBM Watson Visual Recognition.

Microsoft Bing Image Creator helps users generate AI images with

DALL·E but is more versatile and creative. From a text prompt, it generates a set of images matching that prompt in the style the user requests.

PicFinder.ai is an 'infinite image generation powered by AI' and promises to 'get great images with 5+ word descriptions'. It's free, but results are hit and miss.

Stable Diffusion, from Stability AI, allows users to create descriptive images with shorter prompts, incorporates existing images and offers enhanced face generation. It has the advantage of allowing the generated image or an existing image to be edited, but the disadvantage of having to be used via other platforms. At the time of writing, it was similar to Midjourney, which had to be accessed via the social platform Discord, but the latter was planning a web interface.

Search engine optimisation

Ahrefs is an AI-powered search engine optimisation (SEO) tool that helps optimise website visibility and search engine rankings. Features include rank tracking, backlink analysis, content research and auditing websites for SEO errors.

Frase.io is an AI tool that helps with content research and creation, providing relevant insights and suggestions for search engine optimisation. Frase claims it is 'the fastest and easiest way to create content that ranks on Google'.

Sales and marketing

Chatfuel helps businesses build chatbots for Facebook Messenger, and can be used to automate customer service, provide product information and deliver personalised experiences.

HubSpot uses AI to automate its own marketing, sales and customer relations management (CRM). It has also rolled out AI platforms for its customers, like ChatSpot, a conversational CRM bot that helps sales, marketing and service professionals to boost productivity.

ManyChat is a platform that helps businesses build chatbots for Facebook Messenger and can be used to automate customer service, provide product information and deliver personalised experiences.

Salesforce Einstein is a suite of AI-powered tools that helps businesses improve their sales, marketing and customer service. For example, Einstein can be used to predict which leads are most likely to convert, personalise marketing campaigns and answer customer questions in real time.

Chatbots

Amazon Lex is a service that helps businesses build conversational AI applications. Lex can be used to create chatbots, voice applications and other types of conversational interfaces.

ChatGPT is the generative AI service that turned AI into a household abbreviation. The only point to make here is that its creator, OpenAI, is likely to roll-out updates several times a year and to fine-tune the tiers it offers to free and paid users. For business, the paid versions will always be more powerful, effective and cost-effective.

Google Bard is the search giant's answer to ChatGPT and had the advantage initially that it could search the Internet, while its competitor could not. This made it one of the best search engines on the Internet when looking for specific information. However, its propensity to 'hallucinate' and make up information made it one of the worst content generators one could use. Not a single 'fact' it includes in automatically generated articles can be trusted.

HuggingChat is an open-source alternative to ChatGPT and receives contributions from developers on its collaborative AI hub, Hugging Face.

Jasper AI was around long before ChatGPT and was already using large language models before the concept entered the mainstream. However, because it required a paid subscription to get anything useful out of it, the general public never got to hear of it.

Microsoft Bing Chat uses the OpenAI large language model, while also having access to the Internet. It started life with the same hallucinatory flaws as Bard, and its creator continually pulled the plug on various aspects of its functionality. At the time of writing, using it was entirely a hit-and-miss exercise.

General enterprise AI

Cisco Spark Assistant is a service that helps businesses build conversational AI applications. Spark AI Assistant can be used to create chatbots, voice applications and other types of conversational interfaces.

Google Cloud is a suite of services that helps businesses build, deploy and scale AI-powered applications. The platform includes a variety of tools, such as ML engines, natural language processing (NLP) libraries and image recognition interfaces.

IBM Watson is a suite of AI services that helps businesses build cognitive applications. It can be used to analyse data, make predictions and create personalised experiences.

Microsoft Azure Cognitive Services is a suite of AI services that helps businesses build intelligent applications. The services include computer vision, NLP and speech recognition interfaces.

Oracle Cloud Infrastructure AI Services is a service that helps businesses build and deploy AI-powered applications. It can be used to create chatbots, predictive models and other types of AI applications.

Pegasystems provides AI-powered 'decisioning' and workflow automation to solve business challenges, from personalising engagement to streamlining operations.

SAP AI Core is designed to handle the operations of AI assets in a standardised, scalable way and provide seamless integration with SAP solutions.

The efficiency revolution

In May 2022, three of the world's biggest technology organisations unveiled their visions for a future of business that will see a revolution in efficiency.

SAP, the German company that leads the world in enterprise resource planning (ERP) software, search giant Google and chipmaker Intel all hosted major international events, where they launched new products and services and provided a glimpse of the AI-driven future of business.

SAP, in particular, at its annual Sapphire event in Orlando, Florida, signalled an acceleration of efforts to bring greater intelligence to the systems that run organisations' operations.

Google's annual I/O developer conference introduced AI productivity tools that would, among others, provide instant summaries of long documents – six months before ChatGPT came along.

Meanwhile, Intel unveiled a new generation of computer processors that would reduce the time it takes to train large-scale AI models.

But it was SAP that provided the clearest picture of how businesses are likely to operate in the near future. Attending various sessions at Sapphire, I constantly heard the same word: efficiency.

During a keynote address, SAP CEO Christian Klein said that the company planned to draw on data about best practices from more than 40 000 customers. It would leverage Signavio, an enterprise business process intelligence platform it had acquired in 2021, which helps companies transform and manage their business processes at scale.

He told me after his keynote address: 'When you think back 50 years, there's so much knowledge inside SAP and in our ecosystem, we implemented and designed so many business processes, and now we really have our finger on the pulse of how they need to change in a digital world to create a seamless experience.

'We are collecting all of the data, the best practices, not only from SAP but also from all our partners. That's a big differentiator of Signavio: you don't need to replicate data in a third-party data mining tool. You can use your data and then you can benchmark it against how these business processes look in your industry.'

I then asked SAP chief technology officer Juergen Mueller to look into his crystal ball to predict how this capability would change the way businesses make decisions.

'We acquired Signavio for a reason: we saw there's a gap in our portfolio,' he said. 'It's very important to customers to understand the business processes and we've modelled business processes for 35 years or so, but they were often a separate artifact, so your processes are not connected to your execution.

'Signavio gives you an X-ray into your real processes and execution. That has to be the foundation, grounded in reality, from where you then can change, find efficiencies, find how you can do things better, how you can serve your customers faster. Companies often have a good idea where they want to go, but today this X-ray doesn't exist.'

Signavio, however, would allow any size company to access the kind of business intelligence and AI that has enabled tech giants like Microsoft, Amazon and Google to have instant insight into their business processes. From there they have been able to implement a solution and assess its success within minutes, replacing or improving it before most customers know it existed. However, this was not possible without the ability to mine massive amounts of data on the fly. And that ability was previously restricted to the giants.

'We have tens of thousands and potentially hundreds of thousands of other companies that can now get such a detailed level of understanding of their processes,' said Mueller. 'We learn and develop industry-specific best practices in 25 industries, and we can bring the best of what we know to customers.'

The end result, he said, was vastly improved efficiency. However, that in itself was not a differentiator if all companies become more efficient. Efficiency, in effect, becomes a ticket to the game.

But the willingness to embrace tools like AI would become a true differentiator in business.

'We see a huge difference in companies that really embrace digital technologies, and who always want to create differentiating capabilities through technology, compared to the ones that are just using technology where they have to.'

My robot assistant

Allow me to introduce you to a miracle app: one of the few apps that I can truly say has changed my life.

It's called Otter.ai, and it is primarily a transcription app, allowing both voice recording and an immediate text transcription via a web browser. The recording is uploaded to the cloud, and it uses AI to compare words and accents against a vast database. If the sound quality is good, the transcription typically comes out about 98% accurate, but you can read along as you follow the played-back recording and correct as you go. The transcript can then be exported as a text file.

Most of us, from time to time, need to make notes from a meeting, lecture or event, and most of the time we only get a snapshot of what was said. Thanks to the tools available on any smartphone, and when all parties to the conversation consent, we tend to record proceedings and transcribe the recording later.

The problem is that transcription can take four to eight times longer than the recording itself, leading to procrastination or even abandonment of the recording. With Otter.ai, transcription is instantaneous. It is a massive productivity boost.

Here's the real beauty of it: if you record an interview through the Otter app on your phone, it transcribes as you go along. You can even watch the words appear to see which it is getting wrong. On completion, it uploads the transcription and runs it through the same AI software in the cloud, in order to sharpen the accuracy of what it transcribes. It then lets you know when it's ready via notification or email.

You can then activate an edit mode, which allows you to correct the transcription as you listen to the audio. This means that, for example, a half-hour interview can be corrected in half an hour, compared to around three to six hours of manually transcribing a recorded interview. It at least trebled my productivity.

In a Pro version, the user can upload a pre-recorded interview, and it takes less than half an hour to transcribe it in the cloud.

Not only has it saved me many hours of transcription, but it has also ensured I captured everything that was said and never got the quotes wrong. Best of all, during a face-to-face interview, I could now focus entirely on the subject – and have a conversation – rather than have a laptop between us and having to catch up constantly in my typing.

It was, without a shadow of hype, one of my top apps of the early 2020s.

While it can be used in conferences and the likes of court proceedings, the accuracy rate drops substantially when recording from speakers at the other end of a room. It also drops with strong accents, including a range of typical South African accents. However, it does allow the creation of a custom vocabulary.

The bottom line is the quality of the audio, the clarity of the speakers and how close the speakers are to the microphone.

It is free for up to 600 minutes a month, while the power user who needs up to 6 000 minutes a month pays $8.33 a month for the Pro version. This includes Otter Assistant, which automatically joins Zoom, Google Meet or Microsoft Teams links from one's calendar, and it records and transcribes the meeting. It can share live transcripts with all meeting participants, allowing everyone to add highlights and comments collaboratively.

Of course, free alternatives for dictation are built into Microsoft Word,

Google Docs Voice Typing and Apple Dictation. However, their accuracy levels are well below that of Otter.

Made in South Africa: MobileGPT

And now for something completely differentiated. At least, from a geographical perspective.

One of the most convenient AI tools for business is a platform called MobileGPT.

Bear in mind that most AI text models as well as images are trained on content produced largely in the Western world, and the biases of the northern hemisphere dominate – whether cultural or seasonal. Little wonder that, across the African continent, the platforms, services and possibilities that are emerging around the technology seem distant and almost irrelevant.

It was a delight, then, to discover a significant breakthrough in its use emerging from South Africa. Bertha Kgokong, a Johannesburg-based self-taught developer, founded a company called Tati and built MobileGPT as an AI assistant for WhatsApp users. She told me it was aimed at anyone across the globe who wanted to use ChatGPT and other generative AI platforms on their handsets.

I contacted MobileGPT via WhatsApp, and it immediately offered me a menu with a wide range of options, from having a normal conversation with ChatGPT and generating an AI image using Stable Diffusion to generating a formal document like a lawyer's letter or conducting live research via LiveData.

Producing useable AI images proved challenging. Anyone who has used DALL·E, an image generator from ChatGPT creator OpenAI, will know that initial results from such tools can be underwhelming. One must fine-tune the MobileGPT prompt several times to get usable images.

MobileGPT offers a free trial for only 24 hours, after which it requires a $20 monthly subscription fee. That's not expensive – it's the same cost as the Pro version of ChatGPT, but it adds multiple services on top of the chatbot.

The chat option works as well as ChatGPT, since one is not using WhatsApp capabilities but using messaging as an interface to ChatGPT.

I asked it to write a news article about itself, and it told me:

'MobileGPT, a revolutionary new AI assistant for WhatsApp users, has just been launched, promising to provide unparalleled support and assistance to users from around the world.

'This new assistant is programmed to detect the language of each individual user and respond accordingly, making communication clear and effortless. Its knowledge of a wide range of topics makes MobileGPT a valuable resource for anyone who could use a little extra help.

'MobileGPT provides casual, friendly replies with emojis, making its interactions with users welcoming and relaxed. It is always ready to assist users with any task or answer any questions they may have. While MobileGPT has limitations like any AI, it will always direct users to the resources or suggest alternative solutions to meet their needs.

'Overall, MobileGPT is already making significant waves in the WhatsApp community, and it is easy to see why. Its ease of use and expansive knowledge make it an invaluable resource for users from all over the world.'

Of course, a human could have written that with more nuance and creativity, but it does the basic work, much as users have experienced with ChatGPT itself. It's not there to do the job for you but to provide the basic framework or information from which you can build your own work.

Its biggest strength may well turn out to be the access it gives to an AI-powered document generator that produces industry-standard documents like invoices, letters and CVs.

I signed on to the paid version and asked it to provide an introductory article on a business topic for a research project we were about to begin. It produced a highly competent document, which I could use, not in the research report, but to brief my team on elements that needed to be included.

It clearly still has some way to go, as it is limited by the capabilities, permissions and functionality of the AI services on which it draws. However, it is a wonderful example of how the world of AI for business can be leveraged by anyone, and from anywhere.

Made better in South Africa: ChatSME

In September 2023, one of South Africa's 'challenger' banks – newcomers taking on the established giants of banking – entered the AI space in earnest.

TymeBank, through a division called Retail Capital, launched the country's first homegrown large language model (LLM) called ChatSME. Intended to help entrepreneurs grow their businesses, the AI model aimed to provide easy access to knowledge and resources.

I asked Retail Capital brand and HR executive Erin Louw whether this was merely an interface to ChatGPT, since it also drew on OpenAI's LLM.

She acknowledged that ChatSME uses the LLM built by OpenAI, but with a local edge: 'This is Retail Capital's own LLM-powered application that leverages OpenAI's LLMs. ChatSME distinguishes itself by integrating all the content Retail Capital has created and curated over its 12 years – drawing from an extensive library of blogs, white papers, books, survey results, press releases and emails – and that is why it is authentic.'

In short, it would unlock the benefits offered by ChatGPT, Bard and similar technologies, but with more up-to-date information – and more relevance.

'We know that while business owners are idea-rich, they often find themselves time-, resource- and expertise-poor,' said Louw. 'This means they spend their time in their businesses as opposed to on their businesses. These are the people who stand to gain the most from productivity tools like ChatSME for content generation, handling of routine tasks and, importantly, data analysis for making well-informed business decisions.'

Nesan Pather, project lead on ChatSME at Retail Capital, elaborated: 'We are opening Retail Capital's first-hand experience and industry knowledge to everyone, allowing all small and medium-sized enterprises (SMEs) to ask questions, get advice and access tools to help grow their businesses.

SMEs can find resources about managing finances, building a brand or leveraging social commerce tools, all at the click of a button.'

Miguel da Silva, managing executive of Retail Capital, summed up the ultimate benefit of the tool – and of AI in general – for small businesses: ChatSME, he said, was like 'having a dedicated business specialist on speed dial'.

CHAPTER 8

You Can Bank on AI

AI gives South African banks the edge

'Is our banking system really ahead of the American banks?' someone asks me from time to time.

The answer is startling to anyone accustomed to the typical tech narrative – that South Africa supposedly lags between 18 months and 5 years behind technology trends in the United States.

However, in financial services, a very different picture has been evident for many years. The truth is that, compared to South Africa, banks in the US truly are backward, and American companies are complicit in their archaic ecosystem.

While we complain about, for example, an electronic funds transfer (EFT) taking a day or two to reflect in a recipient account, many US-based businesses still insist on making payments via paper cheque, which must be mailed to the payee. For South Africans going to work in the US, or wanting to interact with American companies around payment, it is pure culture shock.

In 2023, we leapt even further ahead, as the South African Reserve Bank implemented a Rapid Payments Programme, which allows instant settlement of EFTs between banks. It is being rolled out under the brand name PayShap and is on offer from even small financial providers.

It may be an overstatement to say we are entering a golden age for South African banking technology, but it's not a stretch.

Hardly a week goes by without some innovation in financial services changing the topography of banking, payments and lending, and AI and machine learning are only accelerating it. First National Bank (FNB) was a pioneer in instant eWallet payments from anyone with a bank account to anyone with a cellphone number. It debuted around the same time as the revolutionary M-Pesa mobile money transfer service was launched in Kenya in 2008 by Vodafone's Safaricom (now owned by Vodacom). However, FNB had already been using cellphone banking for much of that decade.

Pioneering branchless bank Wizzit was one of the first in the world to enable payments via a basic cellphone, using unstructured supplementary service data similar to SMS but with menu and interactive capability. It has taken this and subsequent innovations worldwide.

More recently, in 2015, TymeBank demonstrated, via kiosks in Pick n Pay and Boxer retail stores, how a bank account could be opened and a debit card issued in five minutes. That suddenly became the holy grail of all mass-market banking services. Capitec and FNB promptly enabled quick opening of accounts via a smartphone, using AI and ML. The key to identification was facial recognition technology using standard selfies.

While numerous banks globally use such biometric authentication for logging in, South Africa is a leader in its use for 'on-boarding' new customers.

Michael Jordaan's new Bank Zero uses the same technology but goes a step beyond all others by offering zero-cost banking. Again, it is hard to find an equivalent anywhere in the world.

South Africa's mobile operators are back in the fray after stumbling in their initial launches of mobile money services. In the same month in 2018, MTN shut down Mobile Money and Vodacom closed M-Pesa in South Africa. However, MTN MoMo returned with a vengeance a few years later, using AI- and ML-based biometric sign-on and sign-in, offering a versatile range of services at low cost.

At the same time, Vodacom rolled out a financial services offering via its VodaPay 'super app', offering payment, lending and insurance solutions. The loans suite included VodaLend Compare, Voucher Advance and

Airtime Advance, which function as traditional micro-loans. VodaLend's Cash Advance gives underbanked consumers quick and barrier-free access to funds for immediate needs like emergency doctor visits or topping up prepaid electricity.

The Zapper QR code payment app allows users to make Instant EFT payments at the point of sale, in one click, after linking their bank account to the app. It teamed up with payments application start-up Stitch, it said, to help eliminate barriers to payment for merchants.

All these services have two things in common that provide the clue to local leadership over the US. First, they show a willingness to leverage AI and other emerging technologies in banking, even as the Americans cling to the old ways.

Second, and most significantly, it underlines a comment made earlier in this book: in Silicon Valley, innovation is typically a response to opportunity. In South Africa and across Africa, it is a response to need.

Identity gets a remake

Identity isn't what it used to be. Not only do we have different versions of our identities for different contexts – think ID document, passport and driver's licence numbers all being different, and multiply that by numerous online user names – but we also now enter the metaverse world of avatars and 'skins'. On top of that, AI has come along to provide the ideal tools to replicate identity.

Little wonder that identity verification has become a perilous minefield of identity theft, fraud and fake. Traditional authentication methods can no longer prove that individuals are who they say they are.

The need and demand is clear: solutions that establish a single, trusted identity in the digital age.

Biometrics, like fingerprints, iris scans and even vein detection, are an obvious approach, but they were initially too high-tech to offer a universal solution. Now, they are coming into their own.

'For those who have been marginalised before – as in the banking space

– biometrics provides far more convenient access and verification,' I was told in 2022 by Lance Fanaroff, co-founder and CEO of iiDENTIFii, a South African biometric digital authentication start-up. 'It also reduces the need to travel long distances, not only for banking but also for distance learning.'

For example, students located in remote areas can access online learning, while providers can be sure that the students sitting for the exams are who they say they are – at a level of certainty even greater than in the 'real' world.

The key to the wider acceptance of biometrics as a means of authentication is the pervasiveness of smart devices with cameras, as well as fingerprint identification becoming standard on a broader range of handsets. According to Fanaroff, technology has driven the change, but it is helped along by organisations adopting a shared interest in secure identification and the availability of more databases against which biometric data can be validated.

'Previously, many organisations had to maintain their own identification and verification processes, which was costly, imprecise and prone to exploitation,' he said.

The benefits multiply when one considers the prevalence of AI facial generators and 'deepfakes' that produce authentic-looking videos of a prominent person speaking. AI is also the antidote.

'This is the next frontier,' said Fanaroff. 'Our technology extracts 3D facial recognition, which provides biometric liveliness by simply taking a selfie, cross-matching the data points with those drawn from an identity document, and finally matching the data with government databases, to provide a triangulation of trust.

'Any business that needs to verify it is in business with the right person, a real person and right at that time, needs to be able to assure the genuine presence of an individual online. So that's what we do – we're able to take biometric authentication into a 30-second reality check.'

iiDENTIFii's algorithms and patented light technology are also tailored to ethnic groups, ensuring authentication regardless of geography and ethnicity. It thus meets stringent requirements of regulatory acronyms like KYC, RICA, FICA and AML. It is integrated into Standard Bank's DigiMe, launched in 2020 to create a safe and secure banking experience on a mobile device.

Deployment of such solutions is not without its challenges.

'Many companies may have implemented inadequate solutions and left their key assets, their data and intellectual property vulnerable and at risk. It is well known that the pandemic forced a significant change in many industries, including financial services, telecommunications, health and telemedicine, education, gaming and crypto – all of which hold valuable information that is priceless in the hands of certain individuals.'

An equally significant challenge is poor customer experience. Many of the facial-recognition approaches to on-boarding to a bank are clunky and ask for multiple attempts before they work. The prospective customers often give up before that.

The experience needs to be streamlined, the information needs to be protected and then the identity of individuals associated with that information must be protected. Ultimately, privacy and security is inextricably tied to identity management. And AI is the key to its effectiveness, as well as to the customer experience.

When common sense beats AI

While AI makes it possible to take all these financial services to new levels of efficiency, speed and security, it is not a silver bullet.

For example, much is made of the use of AI in the short-term insurance industry to detect fraudulent claims. In this context, vendors of AI software like to cite its use in the analysis of voice patterns and facial cues in the kind of video submissions that have become commonplace in making insurance claims.

However, the reality is somewhat more mundane. King Price, a short-term insurance company that celebrated its 10th birthday in 2022, said that it found technology and AI more effective for internal than for external use.

'We have tools to measure productivity,' I was told by Gideon Galloway, founder and CEO. 'I can see when a programmer codes or just sits all day long, although our culture was never clock-watching. It was always output-driven and productivity.

'On the efficiency side, it looks at quality assurance. Our IT systems transcribe everything (from calls) and it starts picking up if let's say a consultant is being aggressive to a client.'

Naturally, fraud prevention does enter the technology picture, but not in the way the media hype would suggest.

'We use AI as one of our fraud tools internally,' said Galloway. 'I'm not talking about which claims we reject or repudiate. This tool looks for anomalies. For example, if one consultant keeps passing on to the same consultant on the other side, it says here's something funny, just look at it.

'Then you can look at it and maybe it's normal; that's the normal chain of command, and that's fine. But maybe it's two people colluding. It also picks up anomalies in terms of syndicates, like collusion by panel-beating groups.'

The reality is that AI video assessments are old hat – and not as reliable or even as useful as the hype suggests.

Galloway was unapologetic about avoiding AI in claims assessments: 'We could do photo or video assessments 10 years ago. The submission is still plugged into your back-end IT system, and you make decisions based on that.

'Most of the front-end stuff that you see today is literally just a video that comes to the operator inside the insurer, but the claim is not being decided on the video. A human may be looking at this video, and in the end probably does not even base a decision on the video. They probably phone up the panel-beater to find out more and then do a manual assessment at the end.

'In our early days, there was a panel-beating syndicate that would make chalk marks on the car, and on camera it looks like this car has been in a serious accident and we need to write it off. And then you pick up that it was just chalk, and there's nothing wrong with the car, for example. So there are still flaws in some of these technologies, although obviously technology does speed up the customer journey. But it goes far wider than just videos and photos.'

AI does help to settle claims faster, but that typically happens at the moment the claim is submitted.

'We are already approving claims within a second, so it doesn't even have to take the video into account. I mean, if you're a paying customer and over the years have proven certain things as a customer, the AI tool will decide immediately, and it doesn't really matter what you submitted. We would pay it in a second. It could be your TV, car or anything like that.'

The real secret, said King Price deputy CEO Rhett Finch, was not AI but common sense.

'We settle up to 20% of our claims now within a handful of seconds. A perfect example is a glass claim that comes through and can be assessed quickly, because it's a paying customer who has been around for a long time, and then it's automatically approved. An internal goal is to get that close to 40% for certain claims. It makes a huge difference to the user experience.'

Now meet your robo-advisor

Robo-advisors are effectively made up of an online investment platform that uses AI and a large database of financial advice to personalise both advice and investment strategies for individuals. Key elements of that database are, however, provided by you, the individual.

You start the personalisation process yourself by answering a series of questions about financial goals, risk tolerance and time horizon. The answers are paired with risk profiles and matched to investment strategies that make it appear as if the robo-advisor has created a personalised investment portfolio for you.

The dirty secret of this kind of AI is that your one-of-a-kind advice is really an example of mass personalisation, with little unique to you. Most people fit one of a range of risk or investment profiles, and the most impact new customer information may have is to fine-tune the profiles.

That means that the typical robo-advisor is little more than a matching engine.

The magic begins when advanced algorithms are added, with ML doing the fine-tuning of the profiles, and AI joining in to integrate market information and the user's own life events. This means that a more advanced robo-advisor can keep tabs on both your life and your goals, on the one hand, and the performance of your investments relative to the market, on the other.

As a result, it can continually rebalance your portfolio to ensure it remains aligned with your risk tolerance and financial goals.

There are numerous benefits of robo-advisors over the human variety:

- They charge much lower fees than traditional financial advisers, or at least they should, since you are not taking up a human's 'valuable time'.
- They are convenient, available at any time, and every part of the process is online.
- They can take into account vast amounts of data and information that would be impossible for a human adviser to analyse.
- Their investment advice is tailored to your individual needs, even if it is 'mass-tailored' – it means that an adviser can't bring in human prejudices about you. Well, they can if they are programmed to do so, but any such bias should gradually vanish.
- They can come up with sophisticated investment strategies and help you execute them at a level that is beyond human advisers.

And then there are the drawbacks. Or, as politicians would say, the 'necessary evils':

- You lose out on human interaction and the sensitivity or empathy that is sometimes needed in financial advice.
- In the same vein, they can't (yet) give truly personalised guidance that is based on having had personalised dealings with you over a

long period and knowing the unwritten nuances of your life and investments.

- If a robo-advisor is allowed to make automated investment moves based on market events and 'triggers', it could make highly risky decisions on your behalf, not unlike stock market crashes triggered by programmatic selling.
- Robo-advisors can give bizarre advice if they are allowed to base it on currently trending fads, like one that recommended someone invest in a company that made fidget spinners, because it was all the rage at that moment. Search around and you'll find examples of robo-advice that include investment in pet rock accessories, edible gold and unicorn farts.

The bottom line is not always the line you wanted. Robo-advisors that are given too little leeway may give half-baked advice, and those with horizons that are too wide may promise you the proverbial pot of gold at the end of the rainbow, even if you know it does not exist.

CHAPTER 9

My Doctor, the Machine

The AI will see you now

Healthcare professionals face massive pressure not only to ensure the quality of care but also to come up with new solutions, cures and treatments. As a result, they are increasingly turning to advanced technologies like AI and ML.

But it is hardly a smooth partnership. The issues of skills shortages at the entry level and 'messy data' in leveraging patient records at the high end are merely bookends for a range of challenges.

In December 2020, the annual Amazon Web Services (AWS) re:Invent conference in Las Vegas (see Chapter 7, on the 2017 edition of the event), saw the demonstration of a range of new cloud-based ML tools for health research and treatment.

The tools raised two key questions in terms of global and local relevance, namely how messy data is addressed and how relevant these were to South Africa.

I asked a man at the heart of AWS's health initiatives, Shez Partovi, then AWS director of worldwide business development for healthcare, life sciences and genomics, to explain.

It all started, he said, with ML. And South Africa provided a great case study during the Covid-19 pandemic.

'In South Africa, we have seen how providing access to advanced technologies such as ML is vital to stopping the spread of Covid-19 and helping individuals quickly find medical help when they fall ill. GovChat, South

Africa's largest citizen engagement platform, launched a Covid-19 chatbot in less than two weeks using Amazon Lex, an AI service for building conversational interfaces into any application using voice and text.

'The chatbot provided health advice and recommendations on whether to get a test for Covid-19, information on the nearest Covid-19 testing facility, the ability to receive test results, and the option for citizens to report Covid-19 symptoms for themselves, their family, or household members.'

ML, in particular, was being roped in globally to address the massive volumes of data being gathered from a variety of unrelated sources, he said.

'ML has the potential to serve as an assistive tool for healthcare professionals, providing the support they need to process and analyse the increasing amount of data generated by doctors, hospitals, researchers and organisations, including structured data like electronic health record forms, as well as unstructured data, such as emails, text documents and even voice notes.

'ML is being used in a variety of tasks such as analysing medical images to advancing precision medicine. Tools that leverage natural language processing, pattern recognition and risk identification are also fuelling new models for predictive, preventive and population health and have the potential to help providers identify gaps in care and improve the health of individuals and communities.'

One of the new tools, Amazon Comprehend Medical, was already proving itself. Partovi described it as 'a highly accurate natural language processing service for medical text, which uses ML to extract disease conditions, medications and treatment outcomes from patient notes, clinical trial reports and other electronic health records'.

The beauty of Comprehend Medical is that it requires no ML expertise, no complicated rules to write, no models to train, and it is continuously improving.

It was in use at the Fred Hutchinson Cancer Research Centre, home to three Nobel laureates, where interdisciplinary teams of world-renowned scientists sought new ways to prevent, diagnose and treat cancer, HIV/AIDS and other life-threatening diseases.

Matthew Trunnell, chief information officer at the institution, gave a powerful perspective on its use: 'Curing cancer is, inherently, an issue of time. For cancer patients and the researchers dedicated to curing them, time is the limiting resource.

'The process of developing clinical trials and connecting them with the right patients requires research teams to manually sift through mountains of unstructured medical records to look for treatment insights. Amazon Comprehend Medical can reduce this time burden from hours to seconds. This is a vital step towards getting researchers rapid access to the information they need when they need it, so they can find actionable insights to advance lifesaving therapies for patients.'

In South Africa, the Department of Health has been working to create paperless hospitals in the country.

Partovi spelled out the clear benefits: 'Paper-based clinical records in healthcare facilities result in extended patient waiting times – sometimes between 60 and 80 minutes; reduced quality of care due to files being lost in overcrowded filing rooms; and increased litigation costs. Using Amazon Comprehend Medical, regional public hospitals implemented indexing systems for easier retrieval of scanned patient records.

'Called hybrid e-scripting, the solution enables electronic data storage without typing, an e-sketch pad for electronically accessible medical diagrams and easy-to-use automated pharmacy labelling to reduce medication dispensing time. The impact on implementing this solution was a 90% reduction in patient wait time for fulfilling prescriptions, a 10% reduction in patient hospital wait time and a cost savings of R1 million in software licences.'

And then there was the massive challenge of tracking exposure during the Covid-19 pandemic. History may well record this as one of the great triumphs of AI and ML.

For example, South African start-up A2D24 was in just three days able to develop and deploy an automated AI platform using Amazon Lex for a private hospital group to inform anyone who had been in one of their hospitals of possible exposure to a confirmed Covid-19 patient.

The system automatically sent an alert message and conducted an SMS-based triage where, each day, patients were asked questions about the type of symptoms they were experiencing and, based on the responses, the chat-bot recommended what to do and whether to seek further medical help.

'This application helped to provide critical care to thousands of patients and staff across the country and potentially prevent many new infections,' said Partovi.

A2D24 would go on to develop an electronic medical records application, called Heal, for Netcare, South Africa's largest primary-care medical practice. Designed and built in five months, it was aimed at making electronic medical notes as fast as writing on paper.

By the end of 2022, Heal had generated over four million medical documents, and the company won the award for AWS Design Partner and Industry Partner of the Year across Europe, the Middle East and Africa.

The fundamental issue of messy patient data remained, however.

Said Partovi: 'A challenge to fully realising the potential of ML in health-care is health data locked in unstructured medical text, which makes applying ML time-consuming, costly and sometimes impossible.

'Having patient medical data consolidated into a secure data lake, organised in a standard format, and properly indexed with key entities identified, is key to making this vast amount of information searchable and ready for applying ML learning on top, in order to derive insights and relationships for improving patient care.'

Get that right, and the long-term potential is incalculable.

The next step: Transform healthcare globally

Is it even possible? Some technology leaders are staking their reputation on it.

Fast forward two years, and I am back in Las Vegas, this time at the Oracle OpenWorld conference.

Oracle founder Larry Ellison is not what one might call humble. The founder of the software company and owner of a Hawaiian island, among others, he usually takes to the stage at his company's events to tell the world how much better Oracle products are than those of rivals.

At OpenWorld 2022, however, it was as if a different person had stepped onto stage for the keynote address. While he slipped in references to Oracle's 'self-repairing' autonomous database, he had something else on his mind: transforming the world's healthcare systems.

The need, he said, was urgent. And Oracle could not do it alone.

'The big healthcare technology providers have focused on selling systems to one segment of the healthcare ecosystem – big hospitals,' he said in his keynote. 'So, the hospital buys the system, operates the system and ... each hospital has its own database of electronic health records. Sharing those records is very difficult and your health records are scattered in dozens of databases owned by every provider you've ever visited in your entire life. It's terribly fragmented.'

The current generation healthcare systems, he said, put the health providers at the centre of the system, and not patients.

'That's a fundamental problem. We're going to keep providing hospitals with clinical systems, and we're going to greatly enhance both systems, but we're also going to layer on top of that a national public health electronic record database. Some of that data will want to be shared among nations to provide a worldwide global public health system.'

In short, he said, Oracle planned to build two new public health systems, one national and one global.

'It was made very clear during the Covid-19 pandemic that we are in desperate need of both of those systems if we're going to do a better job of managing healthcare, especially during a crisis.'

It was an ambitious goal, and not one that did not lend itself to humility. But this was not the 2019 version of Larry Ellison.

'We discovered during the pandemic that there's no way we can do this ourselves. We don't have the domain expertise to do this by ourselves. We have to have partners as we automate the ecosystem.

'During the pandemic, we worked with the University of Oxford; we worked with the Centers for Disease Control. We found a number of independent software companies. We had to make our development environment an open platform where they could innovate; they could develop technology that would run on our healthcare platform.'

One key that unlocked the door of possibilities, he said, was a health IT company called Cerner, which Oracle acquired for $28.3 billion in 2022.

'With Cerner's knowledge of healthcare and our knowledge of technology, [we can] merge those together and tackle the next generation of healthcare systems.'

The clue that the goal was not too ambitious, he said, lay in the global credit and financial system.

'They know how much you earn. They know where your kids went to school. They know all of that because there is a global financial base that keeps track of every creditworthy person on the face of the earth.

'Obviously we prioritise shopping way above healthcare. We have no similar healthcare systems, but we know how to build them. We built them for financial records. Why can't we build them for our health records? It's a little more complex, but the answer is obviously, "Yes, we should."'

AI looks into your heart

Now we know what it will take, but we also know that governments are not the best custodians of data, or of our future. But, as individuals, we can do a lot for ourselves that does not rely on government permission.

Or hardly ever does.

On 12 September 2018, Apple unveiled its new Series 4 Apple Watch with advanced heart-tracking capabilities – including an electrocardiogram (ECG) sensor. It had received clearance from the US Food and Drug Administration (FDA) the day before, marking its debut in digital health.

Two years later, in September 2020, its biggest rival in fitness wearables, Fitbit, caught up: it received regulatory approval for ECG on its new Fitbit Sense from the FDA and the European Union's CE mark, which certified that it met safety, health and environmental protection requirements. This meant that, as with the Apple Watch, its app could be used to track users' heart rhythms for signs of atrial fibrillation (AFib).

The third biggest players in this space, Samsung, had received FDA approval for ECG monitoring on the Galaxy Watch 3 the month before.

This was all big news for South African consumers, as the Fitbit has been the most popular fitness wearable in the country in recent years, with Apple and Samsung close rivals. Huawei, also catching up on the technology, has had its smartwatch ECG approved in this country too.

It was also big news for sufferers of AFib, a condition that affects more than 33.5 million people globally. An irregular heart rhythm that increases the risk of serious complications like a stroke, it can be particularly difficult to detect, as episodes can sometimes show no symptoms. Some studies suggest that as many as 25% of people who have an AFib-related stroke find out they have AFib only after a stroke has occurred.

Little wonder that heart disease continues to be the leading cause of death worldwide, despite being one of the most preventable conditions. In South Africa, cardiovascular disease is responsible for almost one in six deaths (17.3%), with strokes the third highest cause.[1]

Now, AI has arrived on the wrist to help cut down this number:

- AI algorithms are trained to identify patterns in ECG data that are indicative of certain heart conditions, enabling smartwatches to provide real-time feedback on heart health.
- AI can detect irregular heart rhythms that indicate AFib, alerting users to seek medical attention.
- AI can personalise ECG monitoring by tailoring the frequency of ECG recordings, the types of arrhythmias it monitors, and the notifications it sends.

'Our ECG app is designed to empower you to assess for yourself in the moment and review the reading later with your doctor,' said Eric Friedman, co-founder of Fitbit, when it announced local availability of the ECG app on its Fitbit Sense smartwatch. 'Early detection of AFib is critical, and … we are making these innovations accessible to people around the world to help them improve their heart health, prevent more serious conditions and potentially save lives.'

He said Fitbit had conducted a multi-site clinical trial to evaluate its algorithm abilities. It tested whether it could accurately distinguish AFib from normal sinus rhythm, generate an ECG trace and record a heart's electrical rhythm. The study showed that the algorithm exceeded target performance, detecting 98.7% of AFib cases, and was 100% accurate in identifying study participants with normal sinus rhythm.

Fitbit had spent two years playing catch-up with Apple, but it took the lead in other areas of personal health monitoring.

The Sense introduced the world's first electrodermal activity (EDA) sensor on a smartwatch to help manage stress. It measured the conduction of electrical pulses in the skin to reveal levels of stress, based on the idea that skin conduction is caused by changes in the sweat glands, which are an indication of stress.

And, of course, AI algorithms pulled together all this information to provide usable insights for the user.

The Sense 2, launched in October 2022, took it a step further with a body response sensor called cEDA ('c' for 'continuous'), which continually monitored stress levels through the day and alerted the user to do something about it when the numbers went through the roof.

In combination with resting heart rate and heart rate variability (HRV) – the variation in the time interval between heartbeats – the Sense used AI to produce a Momentary Stress Detection Algorithm, designed to detect moments of potential stress throughout the day.

That is useful for alerting users to their stress levels as well as building up a history that allows one to discern patterns on one's stress levels. It went another step further by offering stress intervention: on-wrist and in-app ways to help users manage stress in the moment. At a time when mental health was moving to the centre of overall health awareness, the feature could not have been better timed.

It is in another area that the device excelled, however. Most of us are only too well aware of when we are stressed and what stresses us out. But mystery still surrounds our sleep patterns and the behaviours that improve or harm sleep.

Speaking as a sleep-impaired individual, the insights gained from advanced sleep tracking have proved invaluable – not so much in repairing my sleep, but in understanding the factors that impair it.

That kind of insight is the first step to addressing an issue and harks back to my original Fitbit epiphanies: about a decade before writing these words, tracking my steps on the Fitbit Flex became the route to improving my fitness. A couple of years later, the Charge HR started me on the journey to bringing down my resting heart rate. That, in turn, was almost entirely due to combining fitness activity with creating better sleep patterns.

Not all such responses become ingrained habits, though, and the holistic approach taken by the Sense is partly aimed at addressing the difficulty we all have with sticking to health and fitness resolutions. The bottom line is that it leaves no place to hide from the impact of one's own lifestyle.

Yes, you can do AI in your sleep.

AI takes healthcare rural

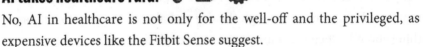

No, AI in healthcare is not only for the well-off and the privileged, as expensive devices like the Fitbit Sense suggest.

It is also being used to develop cutting-edge technologies to improve the country's rural health systems.

To address the issue of limited diagnostic resources in rural areas, the CSIR has developed an ML-powered diagnostics system. The technology combines cutting-edge ML algorithms to help medical professionals diagnose diseases autonomously, and with better accuracy and speed.

The CSIR wants to speed up the diagnosis of diseases, which is often delayed because traditional treatment approaches are reliant on human involvement. By delivering precise and swift disease diagnoses, ML has the potential to reduce the spread of infectious diseases.

On 28 June 2023, a group of young researchers from the CSIR showcased a range of these innovations at a media briefing.

First up was PhD candidate Nkgaphe Tsebesebe.

'The technology can be used in busy medical centres that handle many patient samples each day,' he said. 'With this technology, the diagnostic process can be accelerated, reducing patients' waiting time. It can diagnose thousands or even millions of samples in just a few seconds, which is particularly helpful in preventing the spread of viral and infectious diseases.'

Sipho Chauke, another PhD candidate, demonstrated optical-based biosensor technology for the detection of mycobacterium tuberculosis, or TB. A miniaturised point-of-care device uses light to detect TB bacteria in samples containing nucleic acid.

Its primary objective was to assist healthcare systems in remote areas, particularly rural regions, by facilitating the diagnosis of TB and streamlining the initiation and administration of treatment. The technology aimed to reduce the diagnostic time needed for TB cases, make TB diagnostics affordable and offer large-scale diagnostics of various diseases.

The World Health Organization has an End TB Strategy, which aims to eradicate TB by 2025. The CSIR-developed technology contributes to this strategy through the early detection of TB.

It is an ambitious goal, considering TB is the single biggest cause of death in South Africa.

'Although molecular tests are available for detecting and diagnosing TB, they take several weeks to give a diagnosis and are often expensive to run,' said Chauke. And there were no point-of-care tests commercially available locally to ease the burden of using molecular tests and the costs associated with running them.

'Furthermore, this technology will assist ordinary South Africans by improving early clinical prognosis and treatment initiation for TB, thereby decreasing the rate of transmission and the spread of TB between people, especially in remote settings within South Africa.'

Another device unveiled by the CSIR addressed major changes in the virus genome of both SARS-CoV-2 – a strain of coronavirus that causes Covid-19 – and HIV-1, which leads to AIDS. Both continually see new variants emerge and cumulative mutations resulting in drug resistance. This means there is a need for fast and reliable prediction of emerging mutations in managing the diseases.

In response, the CSIR developed a system called localised surface plasmon resonance, which uses optical biosensors to analyse biological elements, such as nucleic acids, protein, antibodies and cells, without interfering with the molecules in the solution. It is ideal for point-of-care settings, where it offers a shortcut to the usual demand for quick laboratory tests.

The system was showcased by PhD candidate Phumlani Mcoyi, who said: 'With a growing interest in laser-based techniques for point-of-care diagnostics, mutation detection will guide the development of the point-of-care diagnostic system, which will be of particular interest to the most disadvantaged South African communities. The availability of a simple, fast and reliable laser-driven diagnostic technique will reduce the time and costs involved in mutation detection in the health sector.'

In future, ML-powered diagnostics systems will use AI to connect multiple machines between different medical facilities and mobile clinics. This will allow data and scanned images to be transmitted to a centralised database, where AI algorithms can perform diagnoses and send the results back to the facility or directly to the patient.

Once again, these are ML and AI innovations driven by need, rather than merely being cool.

Do try this at home

That is all very well for the future. But what about right now? The good news is, numerous start-ups are working on specific areas of tremendous need.

The bad news is that it is all still very expensive. But with the right investment, it is achievable.

In May 2023, Quro Medical, a healthcare technology company, announced that it had raised a R25-million investment from the

Mineworkers Investment Company (MIC), through its venture capital initiative, Khulisani Ventures. Quro's innovation, it turned out, fitted perfectly with Khulisani Ventures' focus on unlocking the growth potential of scalable and innovative black-owned businesses.

Quro offers what it says are accessible and affordable premium healthcare solutions, through a programme called Hospital at Home. The first of its kind in Africa, the programme allows patients to receive high-quality medical care in their own homes. This, in turn, reduces the risk of infection, while cutting costs compared to traditional hospital stays.

'We're leveraging cutting-edge technology and evidence-based protocols to monitor patient health proactively,' said Quro Medical co-founder and CEO Dr Vuyane Mhlomi.

In other words, AI, ML and connected devices meet the tried-and-tested processes of the hospital world.

MIC impact investment manager Thato Ntseare said: 'Remote patient management is a growing trend globally, and the business case and deep understanding of the value chain presented by Quro Medical demonstrates similar growth opportunities in South Africa. It has high potential for increasing accessibility to healthcare services.'

Quro Medical was established in 2018 by Mhlomi, Zikho Pali and Rob Cornish, and it has partnered with South Africa's largest private hospital group, Life Healthcare. Most South African medical aid schemes pay out claims for its services.

It launched Hospital at Home in 2020, offering clients hospital-level care in their homes. In its first two years, it saw more than 1 000 patients treated in their homes with similar or improved levels of clinical outcomes as in hospitals – and with a better patient experience.

Trust me, I'm a chatbot

Earlier it was mentioned that TB is the single biggest cause of death in South Africa, and strokes are third. Between them, in second place, lies diabetes.

One in nine South Africans are affected by diabetes and, since daily self-management is critical to prevent medical complications, numerous people battle to cope. Uncontrolled, diabetes can result in glucose levels fluctuating and running too high, leading to serious complications, including blindness, kidney failure, heart disease and limb amputations.

A South African healthtech company called Guidepost hopes to address this need with an AI-powered chatbot, launched in May 2023 after several months of trials. It supported patients by providing continuous information specific to their individual challenges, and included personalised coaching. It connected patients with 'diabetes coaches', professional nurses accredited in diabetes education.

Since many medical schemes in South Africa cover only two consultations with a diabetes educator a year, this was a far more significant intervention than a mere chat.

'Over several years, we captured the personal pain points of thousands of patients – where and why they struggle, as well as what customised interventions helped them better manage their diabetes,' said Guidepost CEO Graham Rowe. 'This data informed the development of our chatbot, which uses AI tools to automate complex judgements in the management of diabetes.'

To inform their advice, the human diabetes educators used information from the bot, including data from patients through continuous glucose monitoring devices.

Professor David Segal, chief medical officer of Guidepost, said: 'Doctors and clinicians are not able to micromanage their patients with diabetes daily. This is the gap that Guidepost is addressing to support patients and improve their health outcomes. We provide patients with the tools and information they need to make better choices and better manage their diabetes.'

Said Rowe: 'Based on our initial roll-out to monitor uptake, our chatbot has seen the three-month average glucose levels of more than 2 000 patients drop to within normal levels. This means that we can now extend the solution's presence across South Africa. The bot has proven itself in that our coaches now have the tools at their fingertips to work much faster.

'Diabetes technologies are fast catching up with the exploding diabetes crisis. These include devices, improved medicines, and technology-enabled solutions to help patients better manage their chronic condition.'

Next please

If it sounds as if all our health bases are now covered by AI, we need to drink something healthier than the Kool-Aid that some medical entrepreneurs seem to offer.

Long lines at hospitals, treatment that is either too expensive or non-existent, technophobic doctors and by-the-book medical insurance that allows no nuance tells us that the public experience of healthcare remains rooted in the 1990s. Instead of ensuring that existing hospitals function, government plays both Monopoly and Scrabble with health policies.

But still, the efforts of pioneers, innovators and visionaries continue, and little by little we can see the future of healthcare emerge in South Africa and across Africa, despite all efforts to hold it back.

Aside from what has already been covered in this chapter, these are some of the advances we can expect in the coming decade:

- Prescription guidance: AI will wipe the floor with professional and consumer search engines for ingredient comparison and matching medicines more precisely to patients' conditions.
- Treatment guidance: AI will be used to analyse vast amounts of patient data, including genetic information, medical histories and lifestyle factors to develop truly personalised treatment plans for individual patients.
- Early disease detection: AI is already being used to analyse medical images – think X-rays and MRI scans – to identify patterns associated with specific diseases or conditions.
- Medical research: drug discovery and roll-out will be accelerated, from finding new treatments for diseases to managing large-scale

healthcare data, thanks to AI analysing large data sets of biological data.

Incidentally, I asked ChatGPT to tell me what breakthroughs would result from AI in healthcare in the next decade. It was modest enough to point out that 'as of my last update in September 2021, I can't predict future events'. But it said it could mention these eight potential breakthroughs that were expected at the time:

- Improved medical imaging and diagnostics;
- Personalised treatment plans;
- Drug discovery and development;
- Predictive analytics for patient outcomes;
- Virtual health assistants;
- Natural language processing (NLP) in healthcare;
- Robot-assisted surgeries; and
- Real-time health monitoring.

The real significance of this list lies in how many of these are already part of the healthcare landscape, as seen in this chapter. Robot-assisted surgery sounds futuristic, but it already occurs across South Africa. NLP is as close as the chatbots on our smartphones.

It tells us that healthcare progress is taking place at a much faster rate than the public experience suggests, but also that, even as breakthroughs are achieved, obstacles remain to their implementation.

I liked ChatGPT's unsolicited footnote to the above list. It told me: 'It's essential to recognise that the progress and implementation of AI in healthcare will also be influenced by factors such as regulatory approvals, ethical concerns, data privacy and the willingness of healthcare professionals and institutions to adopt these technologies.'

We knew that long before AI told us.

CHAPTER 10

AI Hits the Road

AI, you can drive my car

It was not meant to be a test drive of an autonomous vehicle. But the Driving Assist button on the steering wheel of the new BMW 330i was just too tempting. The year was 2019, and it was the official South African launch of the new BMW 3 Series.

And there I found myself, on Sir Lowry's Pass near Cape Town, 'driving' with my arms folded, while the vehicle negotiated curves on its own.

Every 10 seconds or so, yellow or red lights flashed to alert me to put my hands back on the wheel. The yellow lights meant the car wanted me to put my hands on the wheel, just to show that I was in control. The red lights meant that I had to take over control from the artificial intelligence built into the vehicle.

With co-driver Ernest Page, we negotiated a major highway, the bends of Sir Lowry's Pass and Hell's Heights Pass (Helshoogte) above the Cape Winelands.

The experience can be nerve-racking for someone who hasn't experienced autonomous driving or hasn't been dreaming of testing it for many years. For this driver, it was exhilarating. Not because the car performed so magnificently, but because it told us just how close true autonomous driving really was.

There was one nervous moment when the autonomous – or rather, Driving Assist – mode disengaged on Hell's Heights. My hands were hovering over the steering wheel as it took a curve. Assist disengaged, and the car began to veer towards the other side of the road. I quickly took over and also sobered up from the giddiness of thinking I was already in the future.

In reality, Driving Assist is part of Level 2 of driving autonomy, one of five stages defined by the Society of Automotive Engineers (SAE).

A presentation on the evening of the test drive by Edward Makwana, then manager of group product communications at BMW Group in South Africa, summed up the five stages as the driver having Feet Off, Hands Off, Eyes Off, Mind Off and, finally, only being a Passenger.

However, the extent to which the Hands Off mode of Driving Assist mimics self-driving, and easily shows the way to Eyes Off and Mind Off, was astonishing.

Let's have a closer look at the six levels of driving automation formulated by the SAE, a global association of engineers and technical experts in the automotive, aerospace and commercial vehicle industries. The SAE levels were first published in 2014 and have been updated a few times.

Level 0: No Driving Automation

The vehicle is manually controlled by the driver at all times. There are no automated driving features.

Level 1: Driver Assistance (Feet Off)

There are some automated driving features, but the driver is still responsible for most driving tasks. It includes adaptive cruise control, lane departure warning and automatic emergency braking.

Level 2: Partial Driving Automation (Hands Off)

The vehicle can control steering and acceleration/deceleration in some situations, but the driver must always be ready to take over at all times. It includes lane-keeping assist and traffic-aware cruise control.

Level 3: Conditional Driving Automation (Eyes Off)

The vehicle can control steering and acceleration/deceleration in most situations, but the driver must be ready to take over in an unexpected situation. This is hands-off driving, but the driver must still pay attention to the road and be prepared to take over at any time.

Level 4: High Driving Automation (Mind Off)

The vehicle can control steering and acceleration/deceleration in all situations, and the driver does not have to be ready to take over at any time. However, this mode is limited to specific areas or conditions, like being allowed to operate only in certain cities or highways.

Level 5: Full Driving Automation (Passenger)

The vehicle controls steering and acceleration/deceleration in all situations, and the driver does not even have to be in the vehicle. Level 5 vehicles are fully autonomous and can operate anywhere that a human driver can.

Most of these capabilities are made possible through remote-sensing technology, including radar, GPS, cameras and Lidar. The latter stands for Light Detection and Ranging, which consists of pulsed laser light to measure ranges. All of these, in turn, operate via complex AI algorithms, ML systems and powerful computer chips. The collected data is processed by AI on a computer, which then decides how to operate the vehicle.

AI in your rear-view mirror

It may sound exceptionally advanced, but much of it has been routine for close to a decade.

Consider the Audi A5 coupé. Back in 2017, it was the biggest smartphone charger I'd ever tested. To most people, it looked like a mere two-door car. But it had one feature I hadn't seen before in a car: a plug-free pad for charging phones that uses the Qi wireless charging standard.

In truth, it was not a big deal and has since become a standard in high-end vehicles. But it symbolised the extent to which the automotive industry was waking up to a future that had already arrived: a future in which the ordering of our lives revolves around handheld devices, and motor vehicles must adapt to these devices.

Like the smartphone, the car must become more intelligent, convenient and supportive of our lives. For this reason, the autonomous vehicle, or self-driving car, is not only a good idea but an essential one. Cars of the future must get us where we want to go, and not the other way around.

It is a standard argument to say that self-driving cars can't work in a country like South Africa, where most vehicles will remain human-propelled for the foreseeable future. However, the argument is slowly being taken out of the naysayers' hands.

The 2017 Audi A5 was a good example. It included not only the lane-assist feature that already alerted drivers of many high-end cars when they were veering out of their lanes, but also 'active lane assist', which steered the vehicle back into a lane when it detected the car moving over the white lines. If the driver was signalling a lane change, the function didn't kick in. But then there was 'side assist', which detected vehicles coming up dangerously close in the next lane – and forced the car back into its own lane.

The main drawback of such features is that they depend on clearly demarcated lanes, which are not pervasive on South African roads. Nevertheless, it represented the arrival of Level 2 autonomous driving in a standard vehicle and did not depend on the largesse of licensing authorities – regarded by many as the main obstacle to the roll-out of self-driving cars, even in the mid-2020s.

It tells you that if you believe self-driving will never come to South Africa, you're already wrong.

You only need look in your rear-view mirror. There's a good chance that one of those cars you see is an Audi or a Subaru or a Ford or a BMW that has an assisted driving feature activated.

As early as the 2016 edition of the Land Rover Discovery, an Autonomous Emergency Braking system could spot potential collisions and apply brakes automatically if an accident was anticipated.

It has a form of self-driving as well, with an off-road feature called All-Terrain Progress Control (ATPC), which allows the driver to hand control over to the vehicle when the terrain is particularly difficult. The driver steers while the ATPC takes over all other functions, including braking, applying torque to the wheels (individually, for maximum traction) and controlling the speed.

In the Subaru XV, launched in that same year, EyeSight Driver Assist Technology comprised two colour cameras positioned near the rear-view mirror. They monitored traffic movement and fed the information to an AI system that fine-tuned cruise control automatically and kept an 'eye' on unintended lane changes. It also featured Pre-Collision Braking, in effect watching for cars that braked suddenly in front or – that perennial South African road hazard – cars cutting in dangerously.

The 2016 Ford Fusion featured the whole bang shoot of automated safety, from Adaptive Cruise Control that slowed the car if it detects traffic ahead to automated perpendicular parking and Park Out Assist for getting out of tight spots. Cross-Traffic Alert was like having a built-in assistant to warn of approaching traffic when a car was backing out of a driveway or parking spot.

The cherry on top was Pre-Collision Assist with Pedestrian Detection, which warned of potential collisions with both cars and pedestrians. The brakes instantly 'precharged' and increased sensitivity for full responsiveness when the brakes were applied – which happened automatically if the driver didn't respond to the alarm.

The 2016 Volvo CX90 featured all of the above, along with City Safety, designed to avoid collisions in slow-moving, stop-and-go city traffic. It braked automatically, avoiding or helping to reduce the effects of a collision.

Every one of the above was a car I tested on the South African roads in 2016.

In the automobile industry, science fiction has long replaced fiction.

It's not a great leap for such features to evolve to fully automated driving as well. The big catch, aside from the law, is that none of the cars are cheap and none are aimed at the mass market. Yet.

In cars, future shock is no longer about how much of driving can be automated. It's about how much of that automation can be built into mass-market cars.

The biggest shock comes when the high-end features like reverse cameras suddenly appear in entry-level cars. The nippy, little Ford Fiesta ST200 may not be a beginner car, but it points the way. It already features rear-view colour cameras for safer reversing and AdvanceTrac, which automatically applies brakes and adjusts engine torque when it detects wheelslip. In 2023, Hyundai released the lower-cost Grand i10 with similar features.

The true breakthrough for the ordinary driver will come when standard features in all cars include lane assist and park assist, as well as the predictive braking systems that appear in high-end vehicles. That will gradually prepare drivers for their next upgrade: the self-driving vehicle, or at least a significant turn of the wheel closer to that AI dream.

Meanwhile, the driving future keeps coming closer. In September 2023, Germany's Federal Motor Transport Authority granted approval for the BMW 7 Series to engage Level 3 autonomous driving at speeds of up to 60 kilometres per hour on motorways.

Self-driving could change the tune of country music

'With the rise of self-driving vehicles, it's only a matter of time until there's a country song where the guy's truck leaves him,' went a meme that appeared on social media a few years ago.

It's a funny line, but it also goes to the heart of our hopes and fears of AI and what happens when vehicles reach what the SAE defines as Level 5. That's when the steering wheel becomes optional, and the concept of a driver disappears.

Already, in Los Gatos in Silicon Valley, cyclists can use an app that lets their smartphones communicate with traffic lights to keep them green for longer. After a while, the cyclists don't even realise it's the phone AI keeping the lights green.

Buses and trucks will enjoy similar privileges. From face recognition technology monitoring drivers to regenerative brakes charging electric cars, to vehicle-to-everything communications, known as V2X, machines will gradually take over. Eventually, the drivers themselves will fade away.

That's when the vanishing trucker becomes as much of a country music icon as the mythical cowboy is today.

This is how it may sound. With apologies to Kenny Rogers and the writers of 'Lucille', (Hal Bynum and Roger Bowling), I wrote the following without AI intervention:

You picked a fine time to self-drive, my wheels (to the tune of 'Lucille')
On a grid in Los Gatos, across from San Jose,
At a charge pad, she went Level 5.
I thought I'd augment her, I navigated to her,
I plugged in to her API.

When the data set hit her, she said: 'I'm no Tesla,
But I finally quit driving assist.
I'm hungry for 5G, machine learning,
I'm after whatever the V2X brings.'

On Facetime, I saw him, I used Rekognition,
I thought how he looked Level 1.
He came to the camera and applied a filter,
He had a strange avatar face.

He was no AI, not even a hybrid,
For a minute my battery went dead.
But our 4G was shaky, his signal was breaking,
He turned to the Lidar and said:

You picked a fine time to self-drive, my wheels.
With four hundred parcels and a bill of lading,
I've had lane warnings, lived through some radar,
But this time your braking won't regen.
You picked a fine time to self-drive, my wheels.

After he faded, and I paid for an upgrade,
I thought how she'd made him backhaul.
From the lights of the charger, to an AWS server,
We self-parked with Azure backup.

She was a robo, but when she processed me,
She must have thought I was ride-share.
I couldn't patch her, 'cos the meme that he posted,
Kept sharing account to account.

You picked a fine time to self-drive, my wheels.
With four hundred parcels and a bill of lading,
I've had lane warnings, lived through some radar,
But this time your braking won't regen.
You picked a fine time to self-drive, my wheels.

Flights of AI fancy

AI and ML have been standard tools in the travel industry for many years, and here we're not talking about autopilot being engaged once a plane is in flight. Rather, we're dealing with the machinations that occur when someone is still looking for flights and trying to find the cheapest options online.

Savvy travellers know they should clear the cookies in their browser between every search for a specific booking. While airlines, agencies and travel aggregators flatly deny it, it is common cause that they can use cookies to track one's browsing history and show them flights that are more expensive, based on their previous searches. If travellers see a price has gone up since the last search, and that it keeps going up after each search, they are more likely to make an impulse booking in case it goes up yet again.

In a different scenario, if your browser history shows you are regularly comparing prices for specific flights, you may start seeing higher prices than someone going in for the first time, based on the thinking that you badly need to buy that ticket.

The US website Consumer Reports put this thinking to the test in 2016 and spent two weeks looking for the cheapest non-stop airfares on five busy domestic routes, using nine popular sites: CheapOair, Expedia, Google Flights, Hotwire, Kayak, Orbitz, Priceline, Travelocity and Tripadvisor.

'We performed four sets of simultaneous searches on different days at different times, for a total of 372 queries,' wrote William J. McGee, who had worked in airline flight operations management for seven years before becoming a journalist.[1]

'To check for merchants offering different prices to consumers based on their computer's browser history, we had at least one tester use a browser with a robust history of searching flights (which would be typical of a comparison shopper) and another using a "scrubbed" browser, or one cleared of all of the "cookies", or data files, that record previous web searches.'

Despite the fact that all the aggregators have access to the same ticket inventories, the team discovered that 'airfares varied as much as $138 for the same route at the same time and as much as $238 over different days', said McGee.

'Among the 372 searches, we found 42 pairs of different prices on separate browsers for the same sites retrieved at the same time (in theory there should have been no differences). In fact, all nine sites provided different airfares on separate browsers at the same time at least once, although it occurred most frequently on Google Flights (12) and Kayak (8). Out of the 42 pairs that differed, 25 resulted in higher fares (by as much as $121) and 17 resulted in lower fares (up to $84 less) for the scrubbed browser.'

While this was not outright proof of manipulation, it is now well established that the best prices will be found when one searches for flights multiple times over multiple days, with and without browser cookies being cleared. If you don't know how to do that, do a Google (or Bing or DuckDuckGo) search on how to clear cookies in your browser.

The bad news is that this is only the beginning of travel price manipulation, and it does not even involve AI. Cookies are small text files stored on your computer in the cache of your web browser when you visit a cookie-using website. New cookies can retrieve information from existing cookies and, in this way, track user behaviour. Supposedly, this is to improve the user experience. In reality, it is most often used for targeted advertising.

However, cookies have no functional ability and are designed purely for information retrieval. It is when AI is roped in to aggregate and analyse cookies that the trouble really begins.

The most common form of AI manipulation of cookies is in dynamic pricing, particularly in travel. Airlines use AI to analyse customer behaviour and adjust prices accordingly.

Google Bard gave me this example: 'If an airline sees that a lot of people are searching for flights to a certain destination, they may raise the price of those flights. This can make it difficult for travellers to find the cheapest flights, especially if they are not aware of how dynamic pricing works.'

It suggested the following tips for avoiding falling victim to its AI cousins in the airline business: 'Use a price comparison website: a price comparison website can help you to compare prices from different airlines so that you can find the cheapest flight.

'Be aware of dynamic pricing: if you see that a flight price is suddenly much higher than it was before, it is likely that the airline is using dynamic pricing. You may be able to find a cheaper flight by searching for flights on a different day or from a different location.

'Use a VPN: a VPN can help you to hide your location from airlines so that they cannot track your browsing history and show you more expensive flights.

'Be careful about clicking on links: if you see a link that says "cheapest flight", be careful before you click on it. The link may actually take you to a page that is designed to mislead you into booking a more expensive flight.'

Of course, since Bard's owners have their own price comparison website, Google Flights, we should even take this advice with a pinch of salt.

It's a start

As I was writing this chapter, a timely email popped up in my inbox: it was from local flight aggregation site Travelstart, announcing 'Africa's first AI travel assistant'.

After checking it was a legitimate proposition, I downloaded the app from the link provided and logged on to my account.

It immediately offered seven examples of the kind of questions I could ask it, including, 'What is the best time to travel to …', 'Book a flight from … to …' and 'Find the cheapest flights to …'

It also helpfully warned: 'This travel assistant is constantly being trained and improved to enhance its capabilities. The responses provided are based on pre-programmed data and algorithms, and there may be limitations or unintended inaccuracies. It is advisable to consult with other sources or professionals for critical travel decisions. Travelstart South Africa or any related entity does not assume any responsibility for the outcomes or consequences resulting from the use of this chatbot.'

Already nervous, I asked for the best price on a flight from Johannesburg to the United Kingdom on a specific date.

It's answer was right out of the ChatGPT rule book: 'I don't have access to real-time flight prices as they can vary based on several factors such as airlines, availability, and time of booking. However, I can assist you in searching for flights. May I know if you are looking for a roundtrip or one-way flight …'

'Round trip,' I responded.

'Great! For the roundtrip flight … I will need a few more details. Could you please provide me with the departure date and the return date in DD/MM/YYYY format?'

Which I then provided.

'Thank you for providing the dates. Now, I'll search for the best available options for a roundtrip flight … Please give me a moment while I find the information for you.'

Several minutes later, I lost patience and asked: 'Have you found anything?'

It again went ChatGPT on me: 'I apologise for the inconvenience, but as a language model, I don't have real-time access to flight information or the ability to browse the internet. However, I can assist you in searching for flights by providing you with a link to our website.

'You can use the following link to search for flights ... By clicking on the link, you will be redirected to our website where you can see the available flights, choose your preferred options and make a booking.'

And we thought AI was changing everything.

What happens in Vegas will be instantly visible

The old saying that what happens in Las Vegas stays in Vegas is being turned on its head by a technology revolution sweeping the city.

Resources like parks and intersections, and services ranging from weather forecasts to emergency services, are being linked by smart sensors to control centres that will allow the city to enhance the living standards of its population.

In the process, vast amounts of data sets will be generated and processed by AI, and what happens in Vegas will be instantly visible to the world. The ultimate aim is making the city more attractive to businesses and residents alike.

That was the vision of Michael Sherwood, chief innovation and technology officer of the City of Las Vegas. I met him during Cisco Live, a conference hosted around the world by global network infrastructure company Cisco. During the Las Vegas edition of the event in June 2022, he told me that the city made for a fascinating test bed for high-tech ideas, and its success stories would be relevant to any community in the world.

'There's always something happening here,' said Sherwood over lunch. 'We have a lot of inflows of people from all over the world, which really gives us a great opportunity to test systems. We have some very interesting and unique weather, from high winds one day to 100-degree weather the next day. So, you know if it works here, it probably will work anywhere in the world.'

Sherwood was not the typical municipal official. He described himself in his LinkedIn profile as 'curator of disruptive innovation'. And he was happy to explain himself.

'Governments are mostly known for slow change, but, to me, disruption is normal. Disruption is good. I like to use disruption for the purpose of providing unique and new opportunities.'

But the outcome he sought was no different to the goal of almost any local authority in the world.

'Cities are in competition to attract people, and the pandemic has shown that you can live and work anywhere. It's a global perspective. We need to come up with things that make Las Vegas unique, that provide our citizenry with amenities and services that they can't get anywhere else.

'If we're going to grow our tax base, which is how we keep government moving forward, we've got to have the right amenities, the right technologies. So, we decided to partner with companies like Cisco to provide innovative and disruptive ideas.'

An example was the introduction of smart parks using AI.

'The ideas behind it may not be super-new, but the way we're applying it is new. People want to feel safe when they're in a park. And the safer a citizen feels, the more often they're going to go visit the park. Cities put a lot of money into operating parks, but don't have any information on how many people use it.'

The solution was to create smart parks, where free Wi-Fi was provided to the community, so that they had broadband when they visited.

'We use that same broadband to power our network systems. We have cameras that allow remote observation of the park, and those cameras also collect data on how many people come in and out of the park – data we've never had before. These systems even identify trash on the ground and issue work orders automatically.'

Other initiatives included licensing autonomous vehicles, 'smart intersections' and 'kinetic streets', where pads beneath the sidewalks generated electricity as people walked over them. The energy was stored in batteries, which then powered streetlights at night.

'The problem we're having with some of these systems is that we have no way of collecting any data out of it. That's where Cisco comes into the network, which becomes the lifeblood of all these different systems. In the next 10 to 15 years, every city is going to need a connectivity platform. We're not going to be late to the party.'

In South Africa, of course, local government is late to every party, even in fixing something as basic as potholes in city streets, thanks to rampant corruption and mismanagement. As a result, the vision of AI-enabled roads and traffic lights is a distant dream. But it shows what AI can make possible if elected officials start thinking about people instead of their pockets or their power.

What South Africa can learn from the Port of Rotterdam

Talking of which, in recent years, South Africa's state-owned rail, port and pipeline company Transnet, has become a byword for inefficiency and mismanagement. Its operations have been disrupted by anything from cybersecurity breaches to strikes, to the inability to overcome congestion in harbours.

During President Cyril Ramaphosa's State of the Nation address on 9 February 2023, he assured the nation that Transnet was 'currently focused on improving operational efficiencies' at the country's ports 'through procuring additional equipment and implementing new systems to reduce congestion'.

'Currently' meant that it would ask for proposals from private partners for the Durban and Ngqura Container Terminals. It could choose to award tenders to the usual coterie of favoured friends, or to the lowest-cost bidder, or – and this would be revolutionary – the best fit for the job, using best practice and best learnings from global case studies.

It was clear that only the latter option would deliver a solution that truly worked. The good news is that great case studies are widely available.

Coincidentally, in that same week, the Port of Rotterdam, Europe's largest port and the world's largest container port outside East Asia, provided media with an unprecedented insight into its technology operations. The tour was again hosted by Cisco, which has helped transform the Port of Rotterdam into one of the most advanced and innovative in the world.

The Port was providing a template not only for implementation of current technology, but also for preparing ports for an AI future.

Internet of Things sensors are located throughout the 105 square kilometres of the port, and a cloud platform collects and processes the massive amounts of data generated. It uses AI to integrate this data with information on around 80 ships entering daily as well as real-time information about infrastructure, water and air. The ultimate aim is to create a 'digital twin', a digital representation of the physical port.

The business and operational ecosystem that has developed around the port draws on the services of a non-profit body called Portbase, which connects the port community across people, companies, systems and supply chains. It ensures the secure exchange of logistics data, improves processes and aims to stimulate efficiency, advancement and innovation.

Donald Baan, Portbase director of business development, marketing and sales, told me during the Cisco tour that ports like Durban had much to learn from Rotterdam.

'They must understand that ports consist of various layers – space, infrastructure, transport, cargo – each with its own challenges, digital maturity and ownership. It is important to create a clear framework for the current state of affairs in each layer and to define ambition levels together with the involved stakeholders. By unlocking the data potential on each layer, ports can be connected to the international trade lanes far more efficiently, which makes them attractive for business.'

The future was not about peering into crystal balls, he said.

'The future of ports will remain more or less the same as currently: hubs for international trade and business, offering a well-accessible, safe and secure space for production and handling facilities to connect with the world via various modes of transport.'

The technology revolution was not about what ports did, but about how well they did it.

'The efficiency, reliability and sustainability requirements of cargo, asset or vessel owners will increase. Thus, ports need to anticipate this and prepare a space and infrastructure to accommodate them. An important part is that data is needed to optimise space and infrastructure utilisation and enable transport optimisation.'

At the same time, much of this efficiency improvement was about advanced technology like AI.

'The most exciting innovations in Rotterdam at this moment are the use of drones, smart infrastructure and digital twins, creating plug-and-play access for digital innovations to access data and implement solutions at scale, and quantum technology and security.'

The most visionary project that Cisco is helping to plan is to enable the seamless admission of autonomous, AI-piloted ships into the port by 2040.

Durban won't need that tech for a while; merely a port that works.

CHAPTER 11

AI Wants to Make Things

AI in manufacture and robotics

As one does, I turned to AI itself to give me a sense of how it may change manufacturing.

First up, Bing Chat gave me two short lists it had found on other websites, which were so generic that they could have applied to any current technology.

As a result, I was startled when Google Bard came up with a list that provided a useful roadmap for the future:

> *Predictive maintenance*: AI can be used to predict when equipment is likely to fail, so that maintenance can be performed before the failure occurs. This can help to prevent costly downtime and improve the overall reliability of manufacturing processes.
>
> *Quality control*: AI can be used to inspect products for defects, even in complex and high-speed manufacturing processes. This can help to improve quality and reduce the number of defective products.
>
> *Process optimisation*: AI can be used to optimise manufacturing processes, such as by identifying the most efficient way to produce a product or by scheduling production to minimise waste. This can help to reduce costs and improve productivity.

Product design: AI can be used to design new products by simulating the performance of different designs and identifying the most promising options. This can help to reduce the time and cost of product development.

Supply chain management: AI can be used to manage the supply chain, such as by forecasting demand, optimising inventory levels and managing transportation. This can help to ensure that the right products are available at the right time, and that costs are minimised.

AI, as it were, speaks for itself in manufacturing. But what about that holy grail of manufacturing: automation?

Here, Google Bard became as dull as Bing, stating the obvious about increased productivity (AI can help to automate tasks that are currently performed by humans, which can free up workers to focus on more strategic and value-added activities) and reduced costs (by automating tasks, optimising processes and improving quality).

A human could have told you that. Actually, humans keep telling us that. So, I went looking for humans who already have deep insights into the future of automated and robotic manufacturing.

Robots are (maybe) not coming for you

As robots migrate from science fiction to the real world, their image as killers has also migrated – but this time the fear is that they will kill off our jobs. The evidence, however, suggests that their effect will be the exact opposite of these fears.

One can go all the way back to the dawn of the Industrial Revolution and the first manufacturing machine: the spinning jenny, which began the automation of weaving. There is one small statistic from that revolution that is seldom mentioned, according to Tom Raftery, former global vice-president and futurist for software giant SAP.

'The spinning jenny was the first mechanical loom,' he told me during a visit to South Africa a few years ago. 'There were 7 900 spinners and loomers in the United Kingdom at the time, in 1760. They had riots, but by 1790 the number of spinners and weavers rose to 32 000, because spinning jennies could make yarn cheaper and better quality than the manual process.'

In fact, the riots were provoked not by the fear of machines taking away jobs, as myth has it, but rather because they brought the price of cotton and cloth crashing down. But that, too, resulted in a boom, rather than the market collapsing, as had been feared.

'Because of increased demand as more people could afford to buy manufactured clothes, economies of scale kicked in, the quality kept increasing and they needed supply chains to supply the factories. For that, they needed distribution mechanisms, and that led to more roads, railways and ultimately the Industrial Revolution.'

In the same way, rather than jobs disappearing as a result of the widespread advent of robots and AI, we will see a process called labour switching.

Raftery quoted a study by Deloitte, which claimed that as organisations embrace and adopt robotics and AI, they are finding that virtually every job can be redesigned, thus creating new categories of work.

Deloitte's 2019 Global Human Capital Trends report asked, 'Are jobs going away due to technology?'[1]

The answer was mixed but reassuring: 'While some may be eliminated, our view is that many more are changing ... only 13% believe automation will eliminate a significant number of positions, far different from our findings on this score only a few years ago.'

The value of automation and AI, Deloitte said, 'lies not in the ability to replace human labour with machines, but in augmenting the workforce and enabling human work to be reframed in terms of problem-solving and the ability to create new knowledge'.

Raftery pointed to some unexpected results of the growing number of skilled jobs and, by extension, better-paid young people.

'Employment in professional services has gone way up, as have numbers of bar staff and the number of hairdressers – as we have more money to enjoy ourselves, as we have more money to improve our appearance.

'New jobs are being created by technology all the time. How many of your job titles existed 5 years ago, 10, 15? More than 60% of the global workforce in 1900 was employed in agriculture and manufacture. Today it is 11%, and we don't have vast unemployment in those areas. Robots won't take our jobs; they will be creating jobs.'

Raftery pointed to five industries – healthcare, manufacturing, energy, transportation and food production – that will be dramatically affected by emerging technologies like AI, big data, robotics and cloud computing. These technologies make up the so-called Fourth Industrial Revolution, a phrase commonly bandied about in South African government circles, but with little awareness of what it truly represents.

Raftery said we can expect to see a decimation of existing jobs in these industries – a prospect that government will find somewhat difficult to sell to the labour unions. However, each of these sectors will see a massive demand for new jobs and skills. Already, the cybersecurity industry, which in effect has to secure the data of every one of these sectors, is reporting a desperate shortage of skills, both in South Africa and globally.

Manufacturing, seemingly the most boring of all industries, will present us with the most fascinating opportunities and challenges.

'We are seeing a move to 3D printing and to mass customisation, which is really product-as-a-service. Fiat is building a modular electric car that one can endlessly customise, down to the battery pack. You can even order an extra 500 kilometres of range for the weekend, getting a more expensive battery just for the weekend when you need it.'

United Parcel Service, an American delivery and supply chain management company, has grasped one of the big opportunities offered by 3D printing of products on demand.

'At present, UPS has a huge business storing parts for customers,' said Raftery. 'They hold US$1.8 trillion worth of customer stock in their warehouses. Now they've partnered with SAP to launch a spare parts 3D printing business. They're going through a certification process with customers to sign off that their 3D printed parts are as good as the originals. Then the products will be digitised and put in a digital warehouse and can be sent anywhere in world.'

Some of the world's biggest technology manufacturers were getting in on the act.

A few years ago, HP formally opened the doors of a massive new 3D Printing and Digital Manufacturing Center of Excellence near Barcelona. It provides a large-scale factory environment to collaborate with customers and partners on digital manufacturing technologies.

During my visit to the centre, Nick Lazaridis, president of HP for Europe, the Middle East and Africa, told me that many companies made the mistake of thinking of the printing industry in terms of sales of printers and materials.

'If you had a total monopoly of 3D printing, the market would be worth around $40 billion. But if you look at the industry that this is going to disrupt, namely manufacturing, that's a $12 trillion industry.'

As with Raftery, however, he predicted that 3D printing would have a massive impact on distribution, warehousing and energy needs.

'This smartphone or bottle is being manufactured in a low-cost country. But you have to build factories, manufacture the products, warehouse them, put them on planes and boats, warehouse them again, and put them on trucks again, before they arrive on the shelves. That leaves behind a massive carbon footprint.

'When you talk 3D printing, you can design in Spain or South Africa, you can manufacture on demand in South Africa, and deliver in 24 hours because it is printed in a warehouse a few blocks from where you live. You don't build a hundred thousand units hoping to sell them; you build on demand,' said Raftery.

Obviously, AI, robots, 3D printing and every other expression of the Fourth Industrial Revolution will kill off jobs. But equally obviously, many of the jobs they create will not only be better jobs, but they could also be better for our planet.

When robots come to save our jobs

When the World Economic Forum declared in 2016 that five million jobs would be lost to emerging technologies like robotics and AI by 2020, the potential for creating new jobs was lost in the statistics.

Three years later, in October 2019, Ford Motor Company showed off a team of 'cobots' – collaborative robots – at its Fiesta plant in Cologne, Germany, to demonstrate how robots allowed engineers to focus on more complex tasks, thus making them more productive.

But it's a lesson that Ford had learned in South Africa almost a decade before. According to Ockert Berry, Ford vice-president of operations for the Middle East and Africa, the ensuing 10 years had seen massive benefits – to productivity and job creation – from the use of technologies we now call the Fourth Industrial Revolution.

'We've always used big data, robotics and AI,' he said. 'It's part of what we do.'

It had a massive impact on the company's ability to compete internationally, contradicting the view that South Africa stands no chance as 4IR arrives.

'When I came back from Australia in 2009, we were producing Rangers in South Africa at $2 700 each, whereas today we are constantly below $1 000 as a result of applying these principles. Within Ford, you compete with other plants for manufacturing business. We competed with Thailand and South America to manufacture cars for the Mexican market. Only if my cost per unit is better will I get that piece of business.'

Berry revealed that Ford South Africa was manufacturing between 40 000 and 50 000 vehicles a year in 2009 at its Silverton plant near Pretoria. By 2019, thanks to maximising the efficiency of both robots and humans, it had a capacity of 168 000 cars and rising. And the impact on jobs was dramatic.

'We only used to work a single shift, about 1 200 people. We did small volumes of every car, only for the South African market. Today we focus on Ranger and Everest and export 80% of what we build to 148 countries. We have 4 500 people on three shifts. And we've brought the cost down per unit in the process. It works when you grow the human and AI side together and both flourish.'

Since all plants have the same advanced technologies at their disposal, the competitive difference lies in the human touch. Berry was lavish in his praise of the South African workforce.

'I've worked now in the US, Europe and Australia, and I will pick our workforce every time. They want to feel they are part of the business. They want to have a voice. If you learn how to do that with them, it is absolute gold. South African workers will do anything for you if they understand what is behind it, the long-term vision.'

Berry said there was no chance of robots taking over completely.

'On a typical day, you will solve 30 to 50 issues, some of which can have 20 to 30 root causes that a human being can identify but that no machine today can do for you. Around 60% to 70% of our automated process will have non-standard work required. There will be subtle differences, for which you can never replace a human applying just the mind to make decisions.'

Where the real robots rule

Every time the Fourth Industrial Revolution comes up in public debate, the emphasis shifts quickly from the opportunities to fears of a future in which robots replace humans. It's not altogether unfounded: hardware robots and the automation of production lines make many human roles redundant, while software bots and streamlined processes are reducing dependence on humans in contact centres.

However, the emphasis on such job losses masks what is really at work: a remarkable increase in human efficiency. Where robots – hardware or software – take over mundane and repetitive tasks, they allow humans to focus on roles that add far greater value than merely following routine. And then, when these bots are roped in to augment human activity, they multiply human value.

That is the holy grail of software robots, better known in the industry as robotic process automation (RPA), and among consumers as bots.

Almost unheard of a few years ago, RPA is now the secret sauce that is enhancing the efficiency of organisations of all sizes.

A company called UiPath was the world's fastest-growing software start-up for three years running in the last decade, thanks to simplifying RPA and making it relevant for both automation and augmentation.

Lenore Kerrigan, who was South African country head of UiPath during that period, said the difference lay in the two kinds of bots made possible by RPA: attended and unattended bots.

'An unattended bot runs a process in the background when something triggers that process,' she said. 'It can be triggered by time, a transaction or handover from another bot. It can be hooked into business processes or enterprise resource planning systems or website responses. It completes the process, then sits idle and waits until something else triggers it.

'The attended bot is about bringing the human into the loop, and it becomes a productivity tool. For example, today we all use spreadsheets in business but, in time, we will use a work bot and a home bot, doing repetitive tasks. UiPath has a vision of one bot per person.'

Kerrigan said international organisations were including bot collaboration in key performance indicators: 'They require a certain percentage of your activity to go through your bot. Your mundane, repetitive tasks should be done through your bot, while you focus on more complex tasks.'

Bots don't always neatly fit into a category: attended and unattended bots sometimes work in tandem, as in call centres when unattended bots hand over to humans, who then deal with a particular process with the aid of an attended bot.

'One insurance company has used an RPA bot, working with humans and an artificial intelligence engine, to drop average call time on a specific type of problem from 6 minutes to 2 minutes. The back-end response used to take 24 hours to resolve the problem; now problem resolution at the end of the call is instantaneous.'

Little wonder that RPA is taking off in South Africa. A research study conducted by World Wide Worx, in partnership with ERP software provider SYSPRO, revealed that use of robotics in South African corporations had increased from 6% in 2018 to 37% in 2019 – primarily thanks to RPA.[2]

The sector with the highest uptake, legal services – at a high of 67% – had been able to reap massive benefits from automating standard, routine and dull processes like searches for legal precedents.

In reality, RPA is merely catching up with the benefits physical robots have been bringing to production lines for decades.

CHAPTER 12

When the Going Gets Tough, AI Goes Shopping

The recommendation engine

It all started with a research paper. Back in 2003, researchers Greg Linden, Brent Smith and Jeremy York published a paper in the journal *IEEE Internet Computing* titled 'Amazon.com Recommendations: Item-to-Item Collaborative Filtering'.[1] Fourteen years later, when the journal was celebrating its 20th anniversary, it named it as the single paper from its publication history that had best withstood the test of time.

The trio happened to work for Amazon.com, and the paper was based on an algorithm that had already been in use for six years, since the early days of the company, to base product recommendations on correlations between products.

The more common approach to recommendations was to look at similarities between customers, but the team discovered that a product focus was more scalable, meaning more data could be processed more quickly and more accurately.

It may sound obvious now, but that's because so much of AI and ML in recommendation engines is based on the concept contained in that paper.

Both the technology and the algorithms keep improving, though. The Amazon Science website, which recounted the above story, added this postscript: 'In June 2019, during a keynote address at Amazon's first re:MARS conference, Jeff Wilke, then the CEO of Amazon's consumer division, highlighted one particular advance in the algorithm for recommending movies to Amazon's Prime Video customers. Amazon researchers' innovations led to a twofold improvement in that algorithm's performance, which Wilke described as a "once-in-a-decade leap"."[2]

The power of such algorithms lies in the fact that they do not rely on a single metric, or a mere customer profile. Amazon.com's personal recommendation engine starts with a customer's past purchase history, mixes in their browsing history and adds their ratings or reviews, just to create an initial profile. The information is then used to build a detailed profile.

Then comes the real ML magic – that profile is then used to make recommendations for products that are likely to interest the customer.

The engine works by first identifying the products that a customer has already purchased or rated. It then uses this information to create a list of similar products that might interest the customer. The engine also considers the customer's browsing history, which helps it to identify products that the customer has shown an interest in, even if they have not yet purchased or rated them.

Finally, the engine also takes into account the customer's ratings and reviews. This helps identify products that the customer is likely to enjoy, based on past preferences, and patterns in the customer's behaviour. This allows the engine to make more accurate recommendations, even for customers who have not purchased or rated many products.

It's obvious where this can go, or at least obvious when one considers all the elements that can go into constructing a profile of behaviour and personal dynamics.

For example, get the customer to give permission for location to be tracked, or to add their social media handle to their account, and we will see engines taking into account a person's physical location or social media activity. Add camera access, and even facial expressions can feed into the recommendations, making them ever more personalised.

The end result? The recommendation you see is far more likely to result in you hitting the Buy button.

The returns engine

It's not called a returns engine, but it should be. When a regular customer tells Amazon.com or Takealot that a product is defective or not what was expected, approval for the return occurs anywhere from immediately to 48 hours later.

When it happens too fast for it to have been vetted by a human, you can be certain AI is at work.

In Amazon's case, it uses AI in a number of ways:

- First, to detect fraudulent returns by analysing a customer's purchase history, browsing history and even social media activity, and flagging patterns associated with fraud.
- Second, to track returns behaviour, like how often a customer returns items, what types of items they return and how long they take to return them, in order to identify customers who are more likely to return items fraudulently.
- Third, by integrating product information, like the product's return policy, purchase date and price to identify returns that are not eligible for a refund.

All of this allows Amazon to offer near-instant returns approval, which multiplies convenience as well as customer satisfaction. From a business side, it increases efficiency, accuracy and fraud prevention.

South Africa's Takealot has almost the exact same process, but it still relies on humans for elements of the approval process.

To start with, AI can check that there are valid return reasons, such as the product being defective, not as described, delivered late or simply that the customer changed their mind.

AI is also used for fraud detection software, which looks for things like suspicious purchase patterns and returns for ineligible products.

All returns are then subject to manual review by a customer service representative, who can often draw on experience or even gut feel to make a call that AI cannot. Yes, it's true: AI is not all-knowing.

Next up from Amazon

On 4 August 2023, Amazon CEO Andy Jassy declared in the company's second quarter earnings call to investors that 'every single one' of its businesses had 'multiple generative AI initiatives going right now'.

He said: 'They range from things that help us be more cost-effective and streamlined in how we run operations and various businesses, to the absolute heart of every customer experience … we offer. It's true in our Stores business, it's true in our AWS business, it's true in our advertising business, it's true in all our devices – and you can just imagine what we're working on with respect to Alexa there – it's true in our entertainment businesses … every single one. It is going to be at the heart of what we do. It's a significant investment and focus for us.'[3]

Having listened to him unveil AI revolution after AI revolution during the annual AWS re:Invent conference year after year, while he was CEO of that division, I know this is not hype. Nor is it the typical placeholder we hear from numerous companies while they decide how to get onto the AI bandwagon.

At the 2018 edition of re:Invent, he had made a prophetic comment during his keynote address: 'Most of the world's knowledge is still locked in documents.'

In response, he said, the company was announcing 'a set of new AI services that allow you to be even more effective in everyday activities'. Bear in mind, this was four years before ChatGPT came along with the same promise.

He then handed over to his 'evangelists' to unveil three products designed to turn cutting-edge artificial AI and ML into a commodity.

Amazon Personalize was designed to simplify both personalisation and recommendation. These functions were possible with an AI product launched the previous year, SageMaker, which used ML to create algorithms. However, it was complex, requiring expert developers and data scientists to personalise automated ML tasks. The new tool reduced both the learning curve and time to deploy.

'For over 20 years, Amazon.com has built recommender systems at scale, integrating personalised recommendations across the buying experience,' said Julien Simon, Amazon's AI and ML evangelist for Europe, the Middle East and Africa. To help all AWS customers do the same, he said, Personalize was 'a fully-managed service that puts personalization and recommendation in the hands of developers with little ML experience'.[4]

The second product, **Amazon Forecast**, leveraged what was possibly Amazon's most powerful secret weapon: time series forecasting, to predict future values of time-dependent data, such as weekly sales, daily inventory levels or hourly website traffic. From simple spreadsheets at the one extreme to complex financial planning software at the other, this function is at the heart of sales growth.

'Such tools may try to predict the future sales of a raincoat by looking only at its previous sales data, with the underlying assumption that the future is determined by the past,' said AWS evangelist Danilo Poccia.[5] 'This approach can struggle to produce accurate forecasts for large sets of data that have irregular trends. Also, it fails to easily combine data series that change over time ... with relevant independent variables like product features and store locations.

'Amazon Forecast packages our years of experience in building and operating scalable, highly accurate forecasting technology into an easy-to-use and fully managed service.'

Finally, **Amazon Textract** was a service that automatically extracted text and data from scanned documents. It went beyond simple optical character recognition (OCR) to identify the contents of forms and tables, initiating a revolution in unlocking the world's knowledge – that same revolution that burst into the public eye via generative AI in 2023.

Retail of tomorrow

While writing this book, I received an invitation to attend Dreamforce, a Salesforce conference in San Francisco that would look at the future of retail and selling. The most intriguing session, from this perspective, was one titled 'Retail's AI Revolution: How GPT Is Transforming Shopping'.

It promised a range of learnings: 'Explore GPT's impact on productivity, consumer experiences, and more in marketing, commerce, service, and stores.'

Every one of the phrases contained in that description speaks for itself to such an extent that one almost does not need to attend the session itself. But, of course, that is where the magic behind the tools is revealed.

Consider productivity. Or, more specifically, products. Generative AI can be used to design new products by generating new product concepts and then using computer-aided design (CAD) software to create prototypes. This would help retailers bring new products to market faster and more efficiently.

Or consider consumer experiences. Among many things generative AI can do is to create virtual try-on experiences for customers. This can be done by using 3D models and computer vision to create a realistic representation of how a product would look on the customer. It would then help customers make more informed decisions about purchases, reduce the number of returns, and – possibly most importantly – get them talking about the experience to friends and on social media.

And then consider service itself. Generative AI can answer customer questions, resolve issues and provide recommendations, based on a large language model's access to vast databases of answers to the same or similar questions and queries. This would obviously help retailers provide better customer experiences and reduce the workload on human customer service representatives.

And this is based only on what is possible today. The advances likely in AI in the future will make shopping even more transformative.

It turned out that almost the entire Dreamforce conference was focused on AI.

'There is no question that this AI opportunity is going to change everything and probably anything, and for all of us,' said Salesforce co-founder and CEO Marc Benioff in his keynote address. 'We can see we can have higher levels of customer success and productivity and growth and transformation and strategy with this new technology. It is going to radically change our landscape. Everything is going to shift at the same time.'[6]

Sam Altman, CEO of OpenAI, joined Benioff in conversation on stage, and reiterated this view.

'In the same way that the Internet and then mobile seeped in everywhere, that's going to happen with intelligence,' said Altman. 'Right now, people talk about being an AI company. There was a time after the iPhone App Store launched when people talked about being a mobile company. But no software company says they're a mobile company now because it'd be unthinkable to not have a mobile app. And it'll be unthinkable not to have intelligence integrated into every product and service.'

Case studies presented during Dreamforce ranged from the American Automobile Association to Heathrow Airport, which said it used digital technologies to create personalised experiences that increase customer engagement and revenue.

South Africa's Standard Bank participated in a session on 'building an agile, secure company', while US-based Esquire Bank said it transformed its marketing organisation into a high-performing content marketing team by leveraging AI and personalisation for hyper-targeted marketing. PepsiCo said it was using it to build better account plans, increase forecast accuracy and develop more strategic in-store activations.

During a press briefing later, I asked Benioff for his response to a common view that emerging markets are not ready for AI due to limitations of infrastructure, skills and education.

'Well, I think no one is ready for AI,' he said. 'You're not alone. Every economy is really just wrestling.

'But then you realise that when we talk about education, the opportunity to provide highly customised, highly personalised, great education for every student, this is like a great threshold moment in the world of education. That's a great opportunity for Africa. But that's a great opportunity in San Francisco too.

'A year ago ... this is not where any of us were. The whole world has changed. It's been amazing. It very much reflects the times and reflects the opportunity, not just for your country, but for every country.'

Prompt your virtual shopping assistants

Want to try the future now? If you're a retailer, there is no end of online resources to guide you in prompting AI platforms to help you in business. For example, AI content creation platform Writesonic offers 20 different categories of ChatGPT prompts for e-commerce.[7]

It starts with prompts for generating e-commerce product names to identify market opportunities and for analysing competitor strategies, all the way through to prompts for e-commerce customer survey questions, product launch strategies and brand storytelling ideas.

A.I. Habit offers three dozen ideal prompts for e-commerce, covering anything from summer campaigns to eco-friendly products.[8]

But what about the shopper? Most online roads lead to the retailer because that is the only category of user who will actually pay for such information. No shopper is going to pay to be told how to shop.

So, I did the obvious, and asked Google Bard and ChatGPT to do it for free. More specifically, I prompted them: 'Please suggest the 10 best prompts that will help an online shopper best fine-tune their shopping choices.'

Both startled me by first schooling me in the kind of information that should be included in a prompt, rather than giving me the prompts themselves.

ChatGPT

It started with a chipper 'Certainly! Here are 10 prompts that can help online shoppers fine-tune their shopping choices':

1. **Define Your Needs**: List down the essential features and specifications you require in the product you want to buy. This will help you stay focused on what matters most to you.
2. **Read Customer Reviews**: Look for genuine customer reviews and feedback on the product. This can provide valuable insights into the product's performance, durability and overall satisfaction.

3. **Compare Products**: Compare similar products from different brands to find the one that best suits your needs. Pay attention to the differences in features, pricing and customer reviews.
4. **Set a Budget**: Determine your budget before you start shopping. This will prevent overspending and help you find the best product within your price range.
5. **Research Brands**: Check the reputation and reliability of the brands you are considering. Established and reputable brands often offer better quality and customer service.
6. **Check Return Policies**: Understand the return and refund policies of the online store. This gives you peace of mind in case the product doesn't meet your expectations.
7. **Consider Long-Term Value**: Think about the long-term value of the product. Sometimes investing a bit more in a higher-quality item can save you money in the long run.
8. **Look for Discounts and Deals**: Keep an eye out for discounts, coupons or special offers to get the best possible price on your chosen product.
9. **Ask Questions**: If the product description is lacking information, don't hesitate to contact the seller or customer support to get your questions answered.
10. **Consider Environmental Impact**: If sustainability is important to you, look for eco-friendly and sustainable products to support environmentally responsible brands.

ChatGPT added: 'By following these prompts, online shoppers can make more informed decisions and find products that truly meet their needs and preferences. Happy shopping!'

Google Bard

'Sure,' said Bard, 'here are 10 prompts that will help an online shopper best fine-tune their shopping choices':

1. What is your budget? This is a critical question to answer before you start shopping, as it will help you narrow down your options and avoid overspending.
2. What are your needs and wants? What are you looking for in a product? What are your must-have features? What are your nice-to-have features? Once you know what you're looking for, you can start to compare different products and find the one that best meets your needs.
3. What are your priorities? Are you more concerned with price, quality or features? Once you know your priorities, you can start to look for products that fit your budget and meet your needs.
4. What are your reviews? Read online reviews before you make a purchase. This will give you a good idea of what other customers think of the product and help you decide if it's right for you.
5. What are your comparisons? Compare different products side-by-side to see how they stack up against each other. This will help you make an informed decision about which product is the best fit for you.
6. What are you researching? Do some research on the product before you buy it. This will help you understand the product and make sure it's the right one for you.
7. What are your guarantees? What kind of guarantees does the product come with? This will protect you in case the product is not as described or if it breaks down.
8. What are your shipping options? How will the product be shipped to you? How long will it take to arrive? This will help you plan your purchase and make sure you receive the product on time.
9. What is the returns policy? What if you're not happy with the product? Can you return it for a refund? This will give you peace of mind knowing that you can return the product if you're not happy with it.
10. What are your payment options? How can you pay for the product? Do you have to pay in full upfront or can you pay in instalments?

This will help you make the purchase and get the product you want.

'These are just a few prompts that can help you fine-tune your shopping choices,' said Bard. 'By taking the time to answer these questions, you can make sure you're making the best possible purchase for your needs.'

Aside from the more cheerful tone adopted by ChatGPT, the two are remarkably similar in their advice. It's almost as if they drew on the same vast database of content published on the Internet over the years. Oh, wait …

The truth is, the more generic your prompt, the more generic the response and also the less satisfying the suggestions. The above is a guide to how to shop, not how to prompt AI to help your shopping. Most of us kind of know how to shop. AI likes to shopsplain because that is what it knows.

Clearly, fine-tuning a prompt is not about simplifying it, but about making it more complex, so that the large language model is absolutely clear on what you want.

For example, render the above this way: 'Give me the 3 best text prompts I can use to find the best price on a product. Call it Product X, and write it in such a way that I can type it into any large language model and get a list of the best prices on Product X.'

Google Bard volunteered:

1. 'What is the best price for Product X?' This prompt will ask the large language model to find the lowest price for Product X from a variety of retailers.
2. 'Where can I buy Product X for the cheapest price?' This prompt will ask the large language model to find the cheapest price for Product X from a specific retailer or location.
3. 'What are the current promo codes for Product X?' This prompt will ask the large language model to find any current promo codes that can be used to save money on Product X.

ChatGPT shopsplained again:

> *Prompt 1: Price comparison*
> Compare prices for the same product across different online stores or marketplaces. Are there any significant price variations and, if so, what factors might be contributing to the differences?
>
> *Prompt 2: Discounts and deals*
> Look for any available discounts, coupons or promotional offers for the product. Are there any ongoing sales events or special deals that could lower the price?
>
> *Prompt 3: Set price alerts*
> Consider using price tracking tools or setting price alerts for the product you want to buy. Are there any websites or apps that can notify you when the price drops or reaches a specific target?

As you can see, ChatGPT is not as well versed in the nature and purpose of being asked to produce a prompt.

Google Bard got it right but felt compelled to promptsplain (yes, I just made that word up – but ask ChatGPT to explain it to you).

The most effective answer, surprisingly, came from Bing Chat. It suggested, simply:

1. 'What are the cheapest online stores that sell Product X?'
2. 'How can I compare the prices of Product X across different websites?'
3. 'What are some tips and tricks to save money when buying Product X?'

The message is clear: when pursuing a specific mission, like buying Product X at the best price, don't rely on only one AI tool or virtual assistant. And when constructing a prompt, don't give up when your first attempt looks like a waste of time. Keep fine-tuning, adding on and redefining, even if the prompt ends up looking like an essay. Those are often the most effective in producing the simplest of outcomes.

CHAPTER 13

That Will Teach the AI

First, don't act surprised

One can probably pinpoint the exact date when a student first used ChatGPT to produce a paper in response to a teacher's or lecturer's assignment: 30 November 2022. That is the date ChatGPT went public, and it is a given that early adopters instantly saw its potential for productivity and time-saving.

Students and schoolkids are among the most aggressive early adopters of technology if the tech is going to save effort and improve grades.

The prophets of doom were just as quick to respond, as they always have been.

Let's pause here a moment to reflect on the early years of the Internet, even before it entered the public domain in 1994 and was confined to academia and the military.

Neil Postman, a media scholar who specialised in the impact of technology on society, wrote in his 1992 book *Technopoly: The Surrender of Culture to Technology*: 'The Internet is a wonderful tool for acquiring information. It is not a very good tool for learning. Learning requires thoughtful reflection, and the Internet is designed for rapid consumption of information. As a result, the Internet is making us more acquisitive and less discursive. We are becoming a nation of know-it-alls who cannot think.'[1]

Sound familiar?

Almost exactly a week after ChatGPT was released, *The Atlantic* magazine ran a story titled 'The College Essay Is Dead'. Author Stephen Marche wrote: 'Natural-language processing presents the academic humanities with a whole series of unprecedented problems. Practical matters are at stake: Humanities departments judge their undergraduate students on the basis of their essays. They give PhDs on the basis of a dissertation's composition. What happens when both processes can be significantly automated?

'Going by my experience as a former Shakespeare professor, I figure it will take 10 years for academia to face this new reality: two years for the students to figure out the tech, three more years for the professors to recognize that students are using the tech, and then five years for university administrators to decide what, if anything, to do about it. Teachers are already some of the most overworked, underpaid people in the world. They are already dealing with a humanities in crisis. And now this. I feel for them.'[2]

Now for the punchline. Marche was not writing about ChatGPT. He was responding to an essay written in May 2022 by Mike Sharples, Emeritus Professor of Educational Technology at The Open University in the United Kingdom. Or rather, it was written by GPT-3, the large language model behind the original version of ChatGPT. The model had been released in May 2020, and licensed to Microsoft in September that year, but it still needed users to be familiar with the concept of an application programming interface (API) to access it.

Sharples used GPT-3 to produce a graduate student essay on the controversial topic of 'learning styles'. He found the essay was adequate. And, he said, the form of AI he had used had 'slipped by unnoticed' and could become a gift for student cheats, or a powerful teaching assistant, or a tool for creativity.

'It's called a Transformer, it acts as a universal language tool and it is set to disrupt education.'[3]

He proved his point with the essay itself and then concluded: 'Students will employ AI to write assignments. Teachers will use AI to assess them. Nobody learns, nobody gains. If ever there were a time to rethink assessment, it's now. Instead of educators trying to outwit AI Transformers, let's harness them for learning.'

The Transformers are now universally known as generative AI, but every other word that Sharples wrote was accurate and prescient.

It took just weeks after the ChatGPT earthquake before institutions began to act surprised. On 12 December 2022, the Los Angeles Unified School District blocked the service. A spokesperson told *The Washington Post*: 'Los Angeles Unified preemptively blocked access to the OpenAI website and to the ChatGPT model on all District networks and devices to protect academic honesty, while a risk/benefit assessment is conducted.'[4]

In the first week of January 2023, New York followed suit. Jenna Lyle, a spokesperson for the New York City Department of Education, told education news service Chalkbeat: 'Due to concerns about negative impacts on student learning, and concerns regarding the safety and accuracy of content, access to ChatGPT is restricted on New York City Public Schools' networks and devices.

'While the tool may be able to provide quick and easy answers to questions, it does not build critical-thinking and problem-solving skills, which are essential for academic and lifelong success.'[5]

The first university institution that I could find to have announced formal guidance on the use of generative AI was the University of Washington. In January 2023, its Center for Teaching and Learning, which supports the advancement of the school's teaching community, issued a set of strategies to 'help instructors think about how to communicate with students, set expectations, and develop assignments that increase students' motivation to develop their own skills and ideas.'[6]

As early in the revolution as they may have been, its guidelines remain solid strategies. They include:

> *Set expectations*: Establish a policy for your course around the use of text generated by AI (e.g., ChatGPT) and communicate this with students through the syllabus and/or assignment prompts. Discuss how you will proceed if you discover that a student has turned in AI-generated work.

Communicate the importance of college learning: Many students are focused only on learning that appears to them to relate to their intended career track, but the vast majority of them will change careers at least once in their lives. Talk with students about how the relevance of your course may become apparent years from now. The skills they are learning will likely transfer to other careers - even careers that do not yet exist!

Acknowledge that struggle is part of learning: Talk with students about how intellectual struggle is an inherent part of learning. Learning happens only when we move outside what we already know. Seeking a shortcut or workaround through AI tools only prevents them from learning. The short-term consequence is that they pay for a benefit they never receive. The long-term consequence is that they miss the opportunity to become better thinkers and more effective writers.

Assess process as much as (or more than) product: Lowering the stakes of individual assignments reduces students' motivation for cheating and encourages them to build their own skills and competencies. Low- or no-stakes formative assessments reinforce the notion that learning is a process and demonstrates to students the value of that learning process.

Design assignments that ask students to connect course content, class conversations and lived experience: It's harder for AI-based tools to effectively connect the dots between these sources of knowledge.

Consider teaching through AI-based tools: Think about how using AI-based tools might facilitate students' learning and prepare them to thoughtfully engage these tools in their personal and professional lives. How can students use AI-generated output to think critically about digital literacy and information accuracy?

ChatGPT's greatest gift: Urgency

If nothing else, ChatGPT injected a sense of urgency into the academic debate. In particular, it dramatically compressed the time frame for Stephen Marche's predictions that it would take two years for the students to figure out the tech, three years for professors, and five years for university administrators to decide what to do about it. These were reduced to hours, days and weeks, respectively.

By 16 January, according to *The New York Times*, 'More than 6,000 teachers from Harvard University, Yale University, and the University of Rhode Island had signed up to GPTZero, an AI text detector created by Princeton University senior Edward Tian.'[7]

Further, reported Kalley Huang, universities were trying to draw boundaries for AI, with Washington University and the University of Vermont drafting revisions to their academic integrity policies so that plagiarism definitions included generative AI.

She wrote: 'At schools, including George Washington University in Washington, D.C., Rutgers University in New Brunswick, N.J., and Appalachian State University in Boone, N.C., professors are phasing out take-home, open-book assignments – which became a dominant method of assessment in the pandemic but now seem vulnerable to chatbots. They are instead opting for in-class assignments, handwritten papers, group work and oral exams.'[8]

At the same time, from 9 to 15 January, Stanford University student newspaper *The Stanford Daily* conducted an anonymous poll on the social media app Fizz, which requires a stanford.edu email to join, asking about ChatGPT use. Of 4 497 respondents, 17% reported using ChatGPT to assist with their previous quarter's assignments and exams.

University spokesperson Dee Mostofi said in response: 'Students are expected to complete coursework without unpermitted aid. In most courses, unpermitted aid includes AI tools like ChatGPT.'[9]

There are several ironies here. Google Bard told me that Stanford was the first university to issue a statement on university policy on ChatGPT, but when asked to point to that policy statement, it was unable to do so.

Bing Chat told me Cambridge University was the first to do so but was only able to point to a statement made in April 2023 that cited findings about student use of the tool in 2022. This should come as great news for universities, who can rest assured that basic fact-checking is likely to expose use of AI, since it is currently not capable of that task.

By the way, the formal response from the University of Cambridge was a statement on its website that said (as of August 2023): 'We recognise that artificially intelligent chatbots, such as ChatGPT, are new tools being used across the world.

'The University has strict guidelines on student conduct and academic integrity. These stress that students must be the authors of their own work. Content produced by AI platforms, such as ChatGPT, does not represent the student's own original work so would be considered a form of academic misconduct to be dealt with under the University's disciplinary procedures.'[10]

Meanwhile, how deep would you like your irony?

It doesn't get much deeper than an investigation by *The Stanford Daily* that exposed the school's president since 2016, prominent neuroscientist Marc Tessier-Lavigne, for publishing scientific papers that included manipulated data.

The university brought in an outside law firm to investigate, and they found evidence of both manipulation and 'serious flaws in the presentation of research data'.

According to *The Stanford Daily*, the 'fudging of results' under Tessier-Lavigne's purview spanned labs at three separate institutions, going back to 2001, and identified a culture where Tessier-Lavigne 'tended to reward the "winners" (that is, postdocs who could generate favorable results) and marginalize or diminish the "losers" (that is, postdocs who were unable or struggled to generate such data)'.[11]

While he was given the benefit of the doubt on knowingly participating in such fudging, there was no coming back from the finding that, given numerous opportunities to correct the scientific record, he failed to do so, nor could he provide adequate explanations.

After claiming repeatedly that the issues in his studies 'do not affect the data, results or interpretation of the papers', Tessier-Lavigne resigned as president of Stanford with effect from 31 August 2023.

You don't need ChatGPT to fudge your research.

But then, it probably won't take two decades to expose misuse of generative AI in academic research. Given the urgency of efforts to improve AI detectors, it will eventually be a case of cheat today, gone tomorrow.

The South African response

South Africa has been in a unique situation in educational policy development for the three decades of its democracy. The needs of a newly minted nation have taken precedence over centuries of conventional wisdom and outmoded methodologies in education.

This does not mean that South Africa has got it right.

In 1997, as part of broad education reform, the Department of Education introduced the policy of outcomes-based education (OBE), which focuses on the learning outcomes students are expected to achieve, rather than on the content they are taught.

There were several flaws in the thinking. For one, it was never clear what learning outcomes should be. For another, it was difficult to assess learning since students were assessed on their ability to achieve the learning outcomes. Which came first, the chicken or the outcome?

Finally, it changed the way that teachers needed to teach, and students learn, requiring the latter to take a more active role in their own learning. We can guess how that worked out.

The one big positive that came out of it, however, was that educators were forced to become more open about teaching and learning methods and resources. It means, in turn, that South African institutions are likely to see some of the more progressive responses to generative AI in the world.

On cue, one of the first universities in the world to embrace rather than reject generative AI was the University of Pretoria. In March 2023, it produced a formal 'Guide for ChatGPT Usage in Teaching and Learning'.

It its preamble, the guide encapsulated the opportunity and the challenge: 'These generative Artificial Intelligence (AI) technologies can be helpful for academics and students, providing personalised and adaptive learning experiences, improving student engagement, and reducing the burden on educators and administrators.

'However, these disruptions have also prompted educators to reconsider their teaching, curriculum, and assessment. It is essential to assess the benefits and limitations of these AI technologies carefully, including potential ethical concerns, and to adapt teaching strategies to ensure they align with the changing landscape of educational technology.'[12]

Thanks to OBE, it was as if the country has been there before.

Because it was so groundbreaking, it is worth spending time on the University of Pretoria document. It outlined the following guiding principles to ensure that the technology was used effectively and ethically:

- *Clarify the purpose*: The use of generative AI like ChatGPT should be aligned with the goals of teaching and learning, and the purpose should be clearly defined. It should be used to enhance learning outcomes and provide additional support to students, not to replace human interaction.
- *Emphasise critical thinking*: While generative AI like ChatGPT can provide helpful information, it should not replace critical thinking. It is important to encourage students to evaluate the information they receive and to develop their own ideas and perspectives.
- *Provide guidance and communicate rules*: Students should be guided on how to use generative AI like ChatGPT effectively. This includes understanding how to interpret the results, how to use the technology to enhance their learning, and how to avoid potential pitfalls. Communicate your rules regarding using ChatGPT in your study guide and explain how to properly acknowledge its use.
- *Ensure transparency*: It is important to be transparent about using

generative AI like ChatGPT with students. This includes explaining how the technology works, what data is being collected, and how it will be used.

- *Respect privacy*: Using generative AI like ChatGPT should respect the privacy of students. Any data collected should be stored securely and only used for the intended purpose.
- *Openly discuss the ethical implications*: Discuss the ethical implications of ChatGPT openly and encourage discussions about its limitations and potential biases, implications on copyright, concerns about labour, environmental impacts, data rights, etc. It is important to critically evaluate the quality of results and to use it in accordance with academic integrity policies.
- *Avoid using personal or confidential data*: To ensure compliance with data privacy laws, it is important to avoid using ChatGPT for personal or confidential data. The model learns from its interactions, which may include sensitive information, and treats it as public domain data.
- *Explain how ChatGPT works*: Explain to your students that ChatGPT generates statistically likely word sequences based on a database and that ChatGPT does not understand, think or reason. ChatGPT is a tool to support learning and not a replacement for their own creativity and thinking.
- *Cross-check information*: Look for other sources and check for the accuracy and credibility of ChatGPT answers. Use ChatGPT as a supplement to other credible sources of information and not as your only source.

I could not have put it better myself. Indeed, I know few who could have.

When the robot goes to class

In practice, it will be as difficult in South Africa as anywhere else in the world to move from guiding principles to AI in action in the classroom.

It will need teachers who are both education-savvy and tech-savvy, university administrators who are open to experimentation and generous in the leeway they give for assessment, and students who are willing and ready to engage with a new way of learning.

My favourite case study that encapsulates these demands comes from Harvard University, where students in one of the institution's most popular courses now have a bot teaching them.

Students who enrol in a coding course called Computer Science 50: Introduction to Computer Science have an AI teacher, based on GPT-3.5 or GPT-4 models – but only as an assistant to the real teacher.

The course, known as CS50 for short, is taught by David J. Malan, a wildly popular lecturer, who happens to have been born in Cape Town.

He told the Harvard college newspaper *The Harvard Crimson*: 'Our own hope is that, through AI, we can eventually approximate a 1:1 teacher:student ratio for every student in CS50 by providing them with software-based tools that, 24/7, can support their learning at a pace and in a style that works best for them individually.'[13]

Malan said that CS50 had always incorporated software and called the use of AI 'an evolution of that tradition'.

A CS50 bot, he said, would respond to frequently asked student questions but will be 'leading students toward an answer rather than handing it to them'.

According to the newspaper, CS50, which had 50 course assistants and teaching fellows (TFs), had been plagued by complaints of overworked and underpaid course staff. Malan said course staff were using software tools to grade more efficiently, and he hoped that AI integration would further decrease the time they spent.

'Assessing, more qualitatively, the design of students' code has remained human-intensive. Through AI, we hope to reduce that time spent, so as to reallocate TFs' time toward more meaningful, interpersonal time with their students, akin to an apprenticeship model.'

He acknowledged that early renditions of the new AI programs were likely to 'occasionally underperform or even err'.

'We'll make clear to students that they should always think critically when taking in information as input, be it from humans or software. But the tools will only get better through feedback from students and teachers alike. So they, too, will be very much part of the process.'

That sounds like the kind of bot a student really needs.

CHAPTER 14

Feed the AI, Feed the Planet

Prepare yourself to come hitchhiking with me on a world tour. I am about to take you from Kenya to Egypt to San Diego to Haifa, as we discover how AI is making a difference beyond Silicon Valley.

The Kenyan woman who used AI to change farming

Back in 2015, Leonida Mutuku was just 26, but she was on her way to being recognised as one of the pioneers of digital technology in Africa.

This was all the more startling in that she had ventured into an area in which technology and innovation had been the preserve of large conglomerates and multinationals.

She founded a small company in Nairobi called Intelipro, which she described as 'a boutique data-science consultancy'. Her profile described her as 'a technology researcher, data scientist, entrepreneur, investor and futurist'. On X (formerly Twitter), she called herself a 'Data Scientist and AI Researcher'.

It all sounds visionary and idealistic, but the combination made a real-world impact on a massive scale. By 2017, more than 25 000 small-scale farmers were using her platform to help plan, finance and sell their crops. The only tool they needed to make the connection was their mobile phones.

In just two years, Mutuku had made waves that were felt internationally. She was invited by cloud computing giants VMware to share the keynote stage at its VMworld 2017 conference in Barcelona. The focus of the event was on the future of cloud computing and data centres. Intelipro used elements of the VMware cloud platform and was highlighted as a case study in how small businesses in emerging markets could make a massive impact.

How did she come so far in such a short time? The superficial answer was that cloud computing makes it possible to scale up a small business to a massive level, in a short time and with limited resources.

But beneath that technical layer lurks a story that is almost an archetype of being an entrepreneur in Africa. It is also the story of the early years of AI being leveraged by those who saw its potential before the mainstream arrived.

Mutuku studied actuarial science at the University of Nairobi, but realised she wanted to do more than crunch numbers: she wanted to make a difference. She enrolled for a Masters of Business Analytics and Big Data at a business school in Madrid, which allowed her to attend classes every six months while she built her business.

Armed with this formidable set of qualifications, she 'slowly transitioned into programming' and began working with the legendary Nairobi technology incubator, the iHub. Coincidentally, I had visited the iHub during her time there but had not met her. As luck would have it, I was able to attend VMworld 2017, and we sat down to chat in Barcelona.

'I was interested in how to use computers to analyse data, and that veered into the big data space,' she recounted about her journey. 'I was working with the iHub, supporting a data science lab, and grew it to $250 000 revenue in one year. I was interested in applying data science in industry, as very few businesses in Africa use data to drive decisions. That was the motivation to start Intelipro, to help small and medium-sized enterprises (SMEs) use data to drive customer demand.'

Intelipro developed automated risk models, using AI to help financial institutions provide credit and micro-financing to SMEs. But it was when she began applying her data science to agriculture that the penny truly dropped regarding the power of big data, the cloud and AI in financing farmers.

'We rolled out this mobile-based platform called eGranary, using USSD short codes. One can access the application from any phone by dialling *492#. When farmers register on it, we verify their identity through their mobile number. They are then able to log the size of the farm, production data, how many cages of seed, how much fertiliser, how much they have paid workers, and so on. It's like a diary for the production process.

'At harvesting time, they log how much they harvested. We include data from the East African Farmers Federation, which represents 20 million farmers, to predict their productivity, based on similar farmers' productivity. We can then see how much to give them in terms of credit for seed or fertiliser.

'In some cases, we don't give them the cash but pay a distributor. So, they apply for a loan, also through the platform, and, if approved, they go to the distributor and collect their seeds and fertiliser.'

At the time, Intelipro was working with soy, bean and maize farmers, but the platform is more broadly applicable. Its magic comes in its power of prediction and the benefits that it can bring to farmers.

'When they are planning to harvest, and we have the data, we can give them a portion of the payment upfront, even before the offtaker – the broker who buys a portion of future production – takes it.'

This was only the beginning of Mutuku's plans for farmers.

'Our current product is supporting them in terms of financial services and getting credit, but where it's going is to help make better predictions from productivity data they are logging. Right now, the individual farmer doesn't get predictive analytics, so the next step is how do we give back intelligence based on what they have logged with us?'

This idea is that the platform will automatically send out alerts, based on what the farmer is tracking, with reminders to apply fertiliser. It will even advise them to try a new or different brand of fertiliser, based on productivity data coming in from other farmers.

Mutuku told me that, ironically, she was no agriculture expert.

'Ultimately, our expertise is in the credit and risk profiling, in analytics, not so much directly in agriculture. But this is close to our hearts because of the impact it has and because we are investing in the lending future.

We're currently in Kenya, Uganda, Tanzania and Rwanda through the East African Farmers Federation, but there are so many people who could benefit across Africa.'

AI is coming after climate change

The United Nations November 2022 COP 27 conference on climate change in Sharm el-Sheikh, Egypt, called for 'a giant leap on climate ambition', among other things. As we know, human beings are not big on giant leaps to protect their planet these days. Perhaps it is time for non-humans to show the way.

The good news is that AI is making massive leaps in managing environmental risk. Combine that with a commitment from most major information technology companies to embrace sustainable manufacturing and operations, and the tech tools for tackling climate change should be ubiquitous.

If it hasn't seemed that way, it is largely due to numerous disparate efforts, platforms and applications that, in themselves, don't make a significant impact. However, more and more of the dots are being joined to paint a big picture.

In 2021, IBM launched an Environmental Intelligence Suite that brought together AI, weather data, climate risk analytics and carbon accounting capabilities. The intention was to help companies streamline and automate the management of environmental risks and operationalise underlying processes, including carbon accounting and reduction, to meet environmental goals.

However, COP 27 showed that even all these tech tools in combination were only part of the solution, said Solomon Assefa, vice-president of IBM Research Africa. An Ethiopian with 45 patents to his name, he headed up the IBM research lab located at Wits University's Tshimologong Precinct in Braamfontein.

'The efforts to solve climate change challenges in Africa are too big for one country or organisation to tackle alone,' he told me after COP 27.

'Partnerships underpinned by green IT technology solutions are key to helping African countries address the effects of climate change and meet their sustainable development goals, including access to clean sustainable energy.

'It will take all of us working together and supplementing each other's strengths to overcome these challenges.'

At COP 27, IBM announced a number of organisations that would join its Sustainability Accelerator, which brought together advanced technologies and an 'ecosystem of experts'. These included the United Nations Development Programme (UNDP) and the Environment Without Borders Foundation.

One of the UNDP projects aimed to increase access to sustainable, affordable and reliable energy in African countries, focusing on 'those furthest left behind'. It aimed to forecast electricity access to better guide policy and investment decisions, using both UNDP's technical knowledge and access to IBM technologies.

In Malawi, an IBM collaboration with Heifer International was developing scalable and affordable digital solutions to equip farmers' cooperatives with weather and crop yield forecasts.

Even natural disasters could be brought under the ambit of AI, said Assefa.

'Floods are a major climate hazard on the continent. To help countries be better prepared to address them, IBM's flood-risk modelling capabilities – that include both AI models and AI-enhanced physical simulations – leverage geospatial data layers, such as soil type, land use and elevation, along with rainfall data, to predict areas at risk of flooding using physical simulations.

'Through our partnership with the South African Agricultural Research Council, we are using these AI-powered weather generator models to help African countries enhance their capability to plan, prepare and respond to extreme weather events and natural disasters.'

These initiatives appeared to be only the beginning of a relentless cycle of innovation to address climate change. Assefa said IBM was not standing still.

'We're using AI and hybrid cloud to accelerate the discovery of climate mitigation and adaptation solutions. We're improving carbon emission performance through optimisation and capture and preparing enterprises for the impact of climate change. We believe our technology and expertise can help companies identify and better understand how their own work impacts on nature, together with the steps they can take to mitigate their own carbon footprint.'

That brings climate change full circle to the business world. It is not only the tech tools that count but also a willingness to use them.

AI fighting fires

In 2020, the University of California's San Diego Supercomputer Center (SDSC) developed a decision-support platform called BurnPro, using AI to help firefighters understand risks and trade-offs quickly and accurately so that they can more effectively manage wildfires. But its origins went back a good few years before that.

At the heart of the technology was a highly specialised computer chip optimised for AI, developed by an Israeli start-up called Habana (no relation to South Africa's iconic rugby player). Founded in 2016 to create world-class AI processors from the ground up, it was acquired by chipmaker Intel three years later and still operates independently.

'We are unlocking the true potential of AI with solutions offering orders of magnitude improvements in processing performance, scalability, power consumption and cost,' Habana said on its website.[1]

Its technology was showcased during a media tour of Israel hosted by Intel in September 2022 to preview its new 13th Generation computer processor. And it gave significant insight into what it takes to run true AI applications.

Habana chief business officer Eitan Medina said that the first question Intel asked customers was what applications they wanted to run on their chips. If AI was only a small proportion of these needs, a regular chip would suffice. However, numerous specific applications demanded something far more specialised – as in SDSC's BurnPro platform.

'We put out a lot of collateral that allows ML developers to take our software and try out their own models,' Medina told me at Intel's main developer centre in Haifa. 'We publish reference models so that, with just a very few lines of code, they target our library and run with it.

'Many customers are using AI for applications that we didn't even think of. They approach us and say, "Hey, we saw that you support this model and now ..." Wow, fighting wildfire, who would have guessed?

'Some things you can imagine. If you support object detection and semantic (image) segmentation, for example, you figure out that if someone uses AI to detect an object in a picture, that is useful for many applications, from retail to automotive to medical.

'But there are things we didn't think of, like in financial systems and risk analysis.'

He described how a complex innovation called a residual network, or ResNet, used for training systems to classify images into hundreds of categories, was deployed by LexisNexis RiskView to assess risk in the financial market.

'Instead of relying on super heavy simulations, they found a combination of a residual network model that allows them to do derivatives and then do risk analysis. And this accelerated the value for their customers. Because we thought that ResNet was a computer vision model, we didn't think about derivatives.'

Computer vision, the branch of AI that automates tasks previously only possible with the human eye, is one of the most widely used forms of AI, applied in tasks now regarded as mundane, like image stitching on smartphones and facial recognition. At the SDSC, it uses satellite images to develop algorithms that determine the best way to contain a wildfire.

The best thing about such use cases is that they inspire further innovative applications that would astonish even the makers of one of the world's most advanced AI tools.

How satellites can save forests

Seven years ago, the European Space Agency launched a satellite called Sentinel-2A into space. The launch was barely noticed, except for anyone involved in analysing images taken from space.

The reason? The satellite carried a camera called a multi-spectral instrument, which is able to capture 13 bands of the colour spectrum. The images provide 10-metre resolution in red, green, blue and near-infrared. This is ideal for identification and mapping of crops, soil and water bodies.

Most significantly, the images collected by the satellite were to be made available to the world at no cost as open-source data. Anyone involved in studying land erosion, crop health, emergencies management and water quality was paying attention.

That included a small band of innovators in Pretoria, who immediately saw the potential. They created a start-up called Swift Geospatial and set to work on new applications of geographic information systems (GIS), which are used to visualise and analyse geographic data.

In November 2022, they unveiled one of the fruits of their labour at an event in Nairobi. They launched the Geospatial Forestry Platform (GFP), combining forestry monitoring and GIS solutions to create easily digestible information and data for the forestry sector.

I had the privilege of delivering a keynote address at the event, but I was certainly not the smartest guy in the room.

That was probably Michael Breetzke, founder of Swift Geospatial.

He told me after the event that, while the underlying system was complex, the goal was simple: 'Modern technology can better help describe the changes on our planet and that information should be more accessible to key decision-makers.

'The ability to provide a larger, more concise data set comprised of applicable information will inevitably lead to greater success in the forestry industry. This would then have a definitive impact on a multitude of industries across the value chain.'

Swift Geospatial partnered on the project with Gatsby Africa, a private foundation established by Lord David Sainsbury 'to accelerate competitive, inclusive and resilient economic growth in East Africa by demonstrating how key sectors can be transformed'. It has targeted commercial forestry and the timber industry of East Africa as an ideal sector in which to create inclusive opportunities and jobs and to reduce poverty.

The GFP was described as 'a collection of individual monitoring modules represented and accessible through easy-to-navigate GIS dashboards pulling data and constructing data from high-quality satellite imagery'.

The platform and its dashboards then allowed for actionable information on forest cover and tree health, which provided what Breetzke calls 'decision-support' for the forestry sector.

The most startling aspect of the platform was that, while it used automation through code scripts, it was not yet relying on AI. This meant that it was at the beginning of an innovation journey, which will allow for increasingly powerful solutions as newer technologies are harnessed.

At the same time, the European Space Agency was intensifying its efforts at enhancing satellite imagery. The Sentinel-2A satellite has been joined by the Sentinel-2B, with 2C set to follow in 2024. The existing satellites enable updating images of the entire earth's land surface every five days, making it as close to real-time as free imagery allows. This means it can be used to map changes in land cover and to monitor the world's forests, lakes and coastal waters. Resultant images of the likes of floods and landslides are then utilised for disaster mapping and humanitarian relief efforts.

The GFP uses the images in conjunction with existing resources, like the Site Species Matching Tool, a GIS-based tool that overlays growing conditions across Kenya and Tanzania – based on temperature, rainfall, evapotranspiration, soil types, soil depth and topographic data – with the growing requirements of different species. It then matches species to ideal climatic areas.

Swift Geospatial also collaborates with Esri, a US-based leader in GIS software, location intelligence and mapping, which uses Amazon Web Services (AWS) cloud infrastructure to provide a geographic approach to sustainability across the globe.

In this context, Swift Geospatial is a case study of a world-leading application of innovation to existing information resources. Now add AI and computer vision to the mix, and imagine what is possible.

For example ...

AI from the air

One of the crown jewels of Africa's AI start-up sector is Cape Town-based Aerobotics, which was founded in 2014 to provide instant analytics to tree-crop farmers. It uses drones equipped with high-resolution cameras, combines the footage with satellite photography and runs the results through ML to analyse the imagery.

It was one of the early success stories of AI, ML and drone technology, according to a case study on the AWS website: 'Monitoring every tree for pests and diseases on a 50-hectare farm would previously take a farmer an entire day. Aerobotics has reduced this to 20 minutes with drone technology.'[2]

The product was built on the AWS cloud, which allowed it to process large amounts of data and work reliably for thousands of farmers in remote rural areas. It used AWS's CloudFront, a global content delivery network launched in South Africa in 2018 to deliver content to farmers more quickly, helping them respond more effectively to imminent crop threats such as disease, pests and drought.

In 2019, Aerobotics announced a R29-million investment from local venture capital company Paper Plane Ventures. In 2020, Naspers injected a further R100 million, part of a funding round worth $17 million, making Aerobotics one of Africa's big start-up winners of the past decade.

At the time of writing, in mid-2023, Aerobotics was advertising on LinkedIn for a business development manager in New South Wales, Australia, a general manager in Fresno, California, and a group accountant in Cape Town. Its AI innovation had truly gone global.

Back in 2018, I asked Benji Meltzer, co-founder and chief technology officer of Aerobotics, how it expected to compete with Silicon Valley. His insights highlighted the opportunity that exists for AI start-ups in general around the world. In the subheadings below, I've allocated my own categorisation of the key learning from each of these insights.

Build out your product before trying to compete

'It is a competitive space, but it's also a huge opportunity. There is a lot of variety in it. There have been a few ways in which we have been able to differentiate. Companies in the US are investing lots of money, but many of them are geared to commercialise quickly,' said Meltzer.

'In South Africa we've been fortunate that we could build the product and add value. We were able to focus our efforts on the product from day one without having to worry too much about competition. In the US, a lot of money has gone to distribution in a crowded market.'

Establish a niche

'We've also focused on a niche, on a specific value-add. Each crop has its intricacies, and we realised we needed to focus on a certain type of crop. That has helped us differentiate the value proposition. It allows us to collect a much larger priority data set, as opposed to competitors working across much wider crops and markets,' said Meltzer.

It's not about the tech

'We're not a drone imagery solution anymore, which is very competitive. We position ourselves as a pest and disease monitoring solution for tree-crop farmers. That's meant we've focused on building an end-to-end solution that farmers can use: from data acquisition – the drone piece – to data processes and analytics, to extract insights from the data, to tools that let farmers do something about these insights.

'First we identify a disease in a farm or orchard, then give farmers a tool to diagnose it on the ground, and decide what to do about it. Other players are often building just pieces of the value chain, whether hardware or software or analytics,' said Meltzer.

Focus on the user - and the value-chain of users

From when Aerobotics started, the core user of product has always been the farmer. The vision of the company is to help farmers better manage risk. Pest and disease monitoring helps them do that directly.

'We also realised that, while data has value for the farmers themselves, there are other stakeholders in the agriculture value chain that are also interested. We looked vertically within the crops we focused on and identified that players like banks and insurance providers would also find value. For farmers, it is useful to manage crops more precisely, for banks it is useful from a lending perspective,' Meltzer said.

'With the data we are providing, we can measure the performance of the farm and how well the crop is doing, down to a granular level, on a tree-by-tree basis. For a bank, taking that information and aggregating it, they can benchmark farmers against other farmers, get a sense of quality of production and can potentially lend more accurately in a data-driven manner. At any given time, they can assess your risk on the ground.

'Having access to this tech, banks and insurance providers can offer solutions to farmers to help them farm more precisely, and thus reduce the risk of lending. It's like a Discovery Vitality model.'

Bots can save the planet

It will come as a surprise to absolutely nobody that consumers are fed up with the lack of progress society is making towards sustainability and social initiatives.

Only diehard denialists and conspiracy theorists still refuse to recognise the effects of climate change, and only the supremely self-absorbed do not understand that increasing human suffering is bad for all humanity.

That consumer frustration has become a business issue. A 2022 study of more than 11 000 consumers and business leaders across 15 countries, including South Africa, found that people wanted businesses to turn talk into action – and they believed technology could help businesses succeed where people had failed.

The study, conducted by Oracle and Harvard professional development instructor Pamela Rucker, found that 60% of South African consumer respondents believed bots would succeed where humans had failed with corporate sustainability.

If that sounds high, consider the response of business leaders themselves: 97% of South Africa's business leaders believed human bias and emotions hurt corporate sustainability efforts.

Consumers said bots would do a better job of corporate sustainability than humans.

Global numbers were similar: 61% of consumers say bots would do a better job of corporate sustainability than humans, and 96% of business leaders believed human bias gets in the way of sustainability.

'The events of the past two years have put sustainability and social initiatives under the microscope and people are demanding material change,' said Rucker. 'While there are challenges to tackling these issues, businesses have an immense opportunity to change the world for the better.'[3]

And it would be good for business: 'The results show that people are more likely to do business with and work for organisations that act responsibly towards our society and the environment. This is an opportune moment. While thinking has evolved, technology has as well, and it can play a key role in overcoming many of the obstacles that have held progress back.'

Two sets of findings from the research highlighted the vast gap between what businesses say and what consumers expect:

- 84% believed businesses could make more progress towards sustainability and social goals with the help of AI.
- 89% believed it's not enough for businesses to say they're prioritising non-financial factors like environmental, social and governance (ESG) issues – they wanted to see action and proof.

Oracle senior vice-president Juergen Lindner warned that it was not a zero-sum game: 'Business leaders understand the importance, yet often have the erroneous assumption that they need to prioritize either profits or sustainability. The technology that can eliminate all the obstacles to ESG efforts is now available and organizations that get this right can not only support their communities and the environment, but also realize significant revenue gains, cost savings, and other benefits that affect the bottom line.'[4]

This isn't exactly rocket science. Why, then, is it so difficult for companies to grasp? Here, too, the research had some of the answers.

Almost all business leaders – 91% – said they were facing major obstacles to implementing ESG initiatives. But no specific barrier leapt out. The biggest challenges were the likes of obtaining ESG metrics from partners and third parties, lack of data and time-consuming manual reporting processes, each cited by about a third of respondents.

Consumers had a different perspective: 42% attributed lack of progress to businesses being too busy with other priorities, and 39% blamed emphasis on short-term profits rather than long-term benefits. Some were decidedly more harsh: 37% believed businesses were too lazy or selfish to help save the planet.

No wonder they thought bots could do better.

CHAPTER 15

The AI Future of Music

By Charles Goldstuck

This chapter represents a unique moment in my writing career: the first time I have collaborated on a book with my twin brother, Charles Goldstuck.

He arrives on these pages courtesy of an illustrious career in the US music industry, where he has distinguished himself as both a business leader and innovator. He became the business partner of legendary recording executive Clive Davis, who is famed for signing the likes of Janis Joplin, Whitney Houston and Alicia Keys. The last was via a recording label called J Records, which Charles and Clive established together, and built into the Bertelsman Music Group.

Charles is also founder of The Sanctuary at Albany, a state-of-the-art recording studio and music academy in the Bahamas, and executive chairperson of TouchTunes Interactive Networks, the world's largest out-of-home interactive digital entertainment network, spanning more than 80 000 locations.

He runs GoldState Music, a private investment firm focused on investing in the music sector. His investments range from recorded music to music publishing and technology.

In the course of his career, Charles had a front-row seat to the digital music revolution and played a direct role in pioneering machine learning in music.

In the year leading up to the writing of this book, we began discussing collaboration on research into AI. It was a natural step, then, to invite him to contribute a chapter on the role of AI in music, past, present and future.

The start of the Digital Revolution

In 1981, on the BBC's emerging technology showcase 'Tomorrow's World', the public got the first glimpse into music's forthcoming Digital Revolution. Kieran Prendiville, the show's host, demonstrated the compact disc for the first time and even went as far as scratching the plastic surface with a rock before playing The Bee Gees' *Living Eyes*.

The compact disc had officially started music's digital era.

By 1985, the popularity and acceptance of the CD reached mainstream market penetration. Dire Straits' *Brothers in Arms* sold a million CDs that year, and it wasn't long before other artists were selling multimillion copies of their albums in CD format.

The Discman, introduced in 1984, and the CD-ROM format, enabling computers to read the discs, further accelerated uptake. The next wave of growth was well under way.

Hundreds of billions of CDs have since been pressed, shipped and sold. The compact disc ushered in a golden commercial age for the music industry. But possibly its most disruptive impact was laying the groundwork for the widespread acceptance of digitally recorded music.

This started a chain of events that would nearly destroy the commercial viability of the music industry and eventually result in the widespread use of adaptive AI.

Napster: The black market for music

By the end of the 20th century, the music industry was enjoying a long period of record profits on the heels of widespread CD acceptance. But a series of converging technological advancements and tailwinds would soon upset this comfortable equilibrium.

The most substantial of these advancements was the development of the MP3 file format. In the early 1990s, German engineer Karlheinz Brandenburg pioneered a compression tool that could shrink audio files into tiny pieces of data without compromising sound quality. The MP3 reduced song file sizes from 32MB to 3MB, enabling consumers to download files faster and store more music on their hard drives.

The music-wide standardisation of the MP3 file format, combined with growing adoption of the Internet, provided Shawn Fanning, a computer science student at Boston's Northeastern University, with the conditions that would bring the music industry to its knees. Fanning developed a music-centric website with a search engine that encompassed peer-to-peer file-sharing: Napster had arrived.

At its core, the app allowed its users to browse each other's digital music libraries, picking and choosing what they wanted to copy from each other at no cost.

In effect, it used a matching engine, a precursor to machine learning, to match a user's search query with an index of users and their MP3 tracks currently online. The Napster server would send the user's computer a list of where to find the requested file, and the user chose which version to download.

The music industry's biggest fear had come true – this was essentially the equivalent of home taping on a grand scale. Napster quickly attracted tens of millions of users. All of them were, in fact, violating existing copyright laws. The era of widespread piracy had begun.

Peer-to-peer file-sharing had a near-instantaneous negative impact on the music industry. According to the International Federation of the Phonographic Industry (IFPI), global recorded music revenues experienced an approximately 50% decline from 2000 to 2010. Few industries have ever experienced such a sharp decline and catastrophic disruption.

During this time, in 2000, my business partner, Clive Davis, and I realised that we needed to embrace the influx of new technology if we were to stay ahead of the wave of destruction engulfing our industry. We had just started J Records, which we described as a 'modern era music company'. This meant that Clive and I worked to complement our catalogue and new releases with this new technology by licensing our repertoire to many of the emerging platforms.

Very few in the industry were supportive of our approach at the time.

However, we were able to generate healthy revenue from this early adoption. More importantly, we developed a deep rapport with the technologists who were reshaping our industry. Ultimately, the entire industry would come to the same realisation.

Meanwhile, Napster as a platform immediately faced a massive wave of backlash from legislators and the industry. In 2001, a lawsuit originally filed by Metallica took down the free version of the app.

Napster shut its doors in 2004, but the damage was done, and the cat was out of the bag. Listeners wanted access to more content, including live recordings and alternative cuts, and desired greater new-music discovery avenues. The piracy wave that came with Napster and continued beyond its demise resulted in a 15-year industry cyclical downturn. By 2010, many believed that the industry would never recover.

In a 2017 interview, Brian Hiatt, a senior writer at *Rolling Stone*, described Napster as 'something close to a celestial jukebox'.[1] His lofty but apt characterisation shows that, despite its flaws and the damage done, peer-to-peer file-sharing platforms provided heretofore unseen listening autonomy.

It was like magic, and consumers would not accept the previous model for much longer.

Apple mobilises music

Peer-to-peer file-sharing platforms were not the only disruptive elements of music's chaotic start to the 21st century.

The invention of the MP3 file made music more portable than ever, enabling a struggling California-based company to 'put a thousand songs in your pocket'. The original iPod was introduced in late 2001 – the first in a series of true game-changing inventions by Apple and the beginning of its growth from a business on the brink of bankruptcy into the world's most valuable company.

The portability, convenience and unprecedented storage capacity of the iPod compounded the pressures on the commercial marketplace for CDs. Mainstream interest in physical formats would go on to decline year after year until vinyl's resurgence in the mid-2010s.

But a new set of frictions emerged in the wake of Apple's disruption.

Apple went on to release the iTunes platform and iTunes Store in 2003. iTunes allowed consumers to purchase individual songs from albums for the first time. Disintermediation of the full album format further eroded the allure of CDs. In effect, iTunes allowed customers to buy only the hits.

Apple's disruptive streak continued with the 2007 release of the iPhone, impacting on how music is consumed and distributed. A year later, it opened the App Store, and the smartphone became the gateway to content. Consumers could now access a nearly unlimited library of music from anywhere, at any time.

Taken together, the increase in consumer demand for à la carte music, initially unleashed by Napster and solidified by Apple's series of innovations, was incompatible with digital download costs, creating a commercial drought that would plague the music industry for another decade.

The streaming (and AI) era begins

By 2008, the IFPI estimated that 95% of all digital music was downloaded illegally. The industry had been driven into a corner by the Digital Revolution.

Stakeholders across the tech spectrum began to explore solutions to a set of parallel problems:

- How to provide a service legally and cost-effectively like Napster?
- With such a massive pool of content, how could personalised recommendations be incorporated?
- How could exploding digital demand most effectively be monetised?

Between 2001 and 2008, several advances, which we can now consider transitory, started to tackle these questions. Rhapsody, the first subscription-based streaming platform, appeared in 2001.

In 2006, Daniel Ek and Martin Lorentzon founded Spotify in Stockholm,

Sweden, and launched it publicly in 2008. It was the first streaming service to offer an all-encompassing catalogue, finally providing listeners with unlimited, instantaneous and seamless access to (nearly) all recorded music in the world.

It was not until late 2016 that global streaming revenues eclipsed digital download and physical revenues. But, after a 15-year drought, the music industry had finally found its answer to piracy.

The streaming era began in earnest.

AI's role in the music industry was still not solidified by the early 2000s, but music's Digital Revolution provided the enabling conditions that led to widespread use of adaptive AI in the mid- to late 2000s, followed by generative AI in the late 2010s. The combination of consumer desire for personalised listening experiences, internet-connected mobile phones, and the growing, disruptive influence of technologists and entrepreneurs provided the tailwinds for AI to take centre stage.

Spotify - pioneer of ML and AI

The ubiquitous appeal of music has provided the industry with a unique position as a guinea pig for the widespread adoption of disruptive technology. It is likely that most readers' first day-to-day interactions with machine learning were personalised song recommendations based on listening history.

In truth, long before mainstream interest in generative AI arrived, streaming platforms had been quietly incorporating AI in the form of ML and deep learning.

My experience with ML started when I invested in a digital music platform called TouchTunes Interactive Networks. We were developing a new digital jukebox with a companion application that would run using cloud computing. That in itself was almost unheard of at the time.

It made sense to find a way of giving users what they wanted, whenever they wanted it. But this was easier sung than done.

Music and its language of song titles, band names and artists represent a completely unique mix of words, unlike literature and dialogue. We needed to build a new weighting system that understood clusters of popularity and the effect of time on a song's likelihood to be played.

News of the day or tour dates, or a release coinciding with a movie or TV show, all change the collective public desire for a particular work in the moment. Using ML, we were able to simulate the effect of these rapid shifts in modern-day consumer demands and focus on what would be popular at the time. Initially developed in 2010, our ML framework became instrumental in powering TouchTunes' search and recommendation engine. It is still used today as a core feature of the platform.

Our initial development work was also informed by the experimentation that was being undertaken by companies like Netflix, with its content search engine, and Amazon, with its product search efforts.

Spotify, now the leader among streaming services, has led the charge. It has long considered itself an AI-native platform and, in 2019, the company's vice-president of engineering declared: 'Machine Learning is at the heart of everything we do at Spotify'.[2]

Let's look under the hood.

Spotify uses AI to analyse user data and personalise recommendations in a few key ways.

First, it leverages ML to analyse user data, such as listening history, playlist creation and platform interaction, to predict what a user might want to listen to next. It also uses collaborative filtering, a method that compares a user's behavioural trends with those of similar users. Popular features, such as 'Discover Weekly', 'Release Radar' and 'Yearly Wrapped', also rely on AI to present users with customised playlists based on their search and listening history.

Spotify uses natural language processing (NLP) in its search feature to enhance the user experience and provide more accurate results. Previously, users had to type exact words into the search bar to match content to queries. This approach was limited, as it could only match terms very close to those used in a song, album or podcast title.

With the introduction of NLP, Spotify's search feature has become more advanced and user-friendly. NLP allows the search feature to understand synonyms for different words, paraphrasing and any content that means the same thing as what you searched. This means that searches don't have to be as specific to produce accurate results, enabling users to better navigate the vast catalogue.

Spotify's models are mainly built on reinforcement learning standards, with a simple goal: long-term user satisfaction. The listener's behaviour while playing a particular song is analysed to make predictions and deduce sustainable, diverse and fulfilling recommendations.

This includes evaluating both historic and current listening behaviours, such as songs skipped, songs played all the way through, and songs played most often. The goal is to nudge users towards options that will make them more satisfied and keep them coming back to Spotify.

Interestingly, all of this is done at the user level, making Spotify not a single product but millions of individualised products, which would not be possible without the use of AI.

Spotify's embrace of AI is a major factor in its position as the undisputed streaming leader. All major streaming platforms now incorporate similar forms of adaptive AI in their personalisation engines, allowing listeners to sift comfortably through the vast 'celestial jukebox'.

I would argue that adaptive AI played a significant role in piracy reduction by satisfying the consumer demand that was activated by peer-to-peer file-sharing platforms.

Adaptive AI helped save the music industry: Will generative AI destroy it?

With the emergence of user-friendly, prompt-based platforms, generative AI has dominated the public consciousness since the early 2020s. But algorithmically generated music has been a topic of research and contention among creators since its inception in the 1950s.

The first attempts at computer-generated music appeared in the 1950s with an emphasis on algorithmic music creation. The advent of computer-generated music by pioneers like Alan Turing, with the Manchester Mark II computer, opened many possibilities for musical intelligence research, showing that computer systems could recognise, create and analyse music. In 1957, the world heard the first work to be composed entirely by AI: *Illiac Suite for String Quartet*.

In the decades leading up to the modern music era, the focus has shifted from creating simpler algorithms to generative models. This change can be interpreted as an evolution from musical robotics to musical intelligence.

The musical robot is like the early experiments of the 1950s and 1960s – it could recognise patterns and define specific musical elements but required human knowledge and oversight to determine what sounded 'good'. Musical intelligence, on the other hand, replaced the need for human intervention with a knowledge-based understanding system, and with its own perception of how musical elements work.

In the 1980s, David Cope, a composer and professor at the University of California at Santa Cruz, argued that the scope of computer composition could include a deeper understanding of music. His belief was rooted in a somewhat pessimistic view of songwriting, stemming from the idea that all music was inspired plagiarism. Or, as famed composer Igor Stravinsky once put it, 'good composers borrow, great ones steal'.

Cope went on to develop the Experiments in Musical Intelligence (EMI) analysis program. Instead of brute force composition, EMI was able to compose 'new examples of music in the style of the music in its database without replicating any of those pieces exactly'.[3]

The program was able to deconstruct a musical work into separate parts, classify the deconstructed parts into genres and identify unique stylistic elements. And, finally, it was able to combine compatible musical elements into new compositions, based on the initial input. Cope's revolutionary use of training data is the foundation for many current generative AI music platforms.

How do they work?

At a basic level, modern generative models first encode existing music and its attributes into a database. This is the model training phase. Next, a set of compatible segments are extracted using pattern matching and recognition systems. From there, the musical segments are classified and reconstructed into a logical musical order, using augmented transition networks, until a new musical output is generated.

It is as complex as it sounds. However, as AI technology became more prevalent in the early 21st century, sophisticated players like Google, Sony and OpenAI have developed generative music models, exponentially increasing its accessibility and adoption.

Now, the opening of the AI floodgates threatens to overwhelm the current streaming model. It has lowered the barrier to music creation, opened the door to new monetisation opportunities for creators, and reignited debates around intellectual property and ownership.

To highlight the contentious range of opportunities and risks that generative AI poses to the music industry, let's look at some of the leading platforms, uses and case studies.

Opportunity for creators

From the electropop darling, Grimes, to the legendary Sir Paul McCartney, A-list musicians have leveraged generative AI models to unlock new monetisation avenues, promote deeper collaboration with fans and recreate the voices of long-deceased artists.

Grimes, known for her experimental brand of pop music and use of emerging technology, was the first major artist to develop a collaborative framework to monetise a generative AI model trained with her voice. Her AI tool, called Elf.Tech, allows creators to transform their own voice samples into a 'GrimesAI voiceprint' that can be used in original songs.

The tool was developed using a generative AI music operating system developed by CreateSafe, which was trained using Grimes' voice. Grimes has encouraged fans and other artists to use this AI-generated version of her voice to create and distribute their own songs. She has even offered to split 50% of the royalties on any successful AI-generated song that uses her voice. This unique approach has led to the creation of several hundred songs.

Paul McCartney has used AI to create what he calls 'the last Beatles record'. The AI technology was used to isolate John Lennon's vocals from an old cassette tape demo, enabling McCartney to complete a partial song.

McCartney has also leveraged something called machine assisted learning (MAL), which uses neural networks to identify and isolate individual audio elements, such as voices and musical instruments. In addition to completing 'the last Beatles record', McCartney leveraged MAL technology to virtually duet with Lennon's isolated vocals on a 2023 tour.

AI 'resurrection' has also been used to compose 'new' songs from deceased artists. 'To draw attention to the music industry's mental health crisis', creative agency Rethink worked with non-profit Over the Bridge to create new songs by legendary artists like Amy Winehouse, Jimi Hendrix, Jim Morrison and Kurt Cobain.

Such projects have sparked debate around consent, name, image and likeness rights, and the ethical ramifications of vocal recreation. Yet, there is an undeniable appeal in hearing new releases from favourite artists who are no longer with us.

The innovative titan of K-Pop (Korea-Pop), a company called HYBE, is unsurprisingly at the cutting edge of novel generative AI applications. In partnership with Endel, one of the first consumer-facing generative music platforms, HYBE artist MIDNATT released the first-ever multilingual track produced in Korean, English, Japanese, Chinese, Spanish and Vietnamese. Generative AI turned what would normally be a tedious process in the studio into a replicable, revenue-generating framework to introduce artists into new markets and capture more listeners.

Another lauded benefit of generative AI is its ability to augment the creative writing process. AI chatbots have been leveraged to create lyric ideas and assist with writer's block. Alternative rock band Weezer released a song in 2022, 'I Want a Dog', with lyrics written by GPT-3.

Similarly, prompt-based generative music platforms, such as Google's MusicLM and Boomy, can inspire riffs, hooks and chord progressions, for example. According to an artist survey conducted by MIDiA, a leading entertainment research firm, over 50% of respondents strongly or somewhat agree that AI can be a useful tool for making music. Only 25% disagreed, while 25% were neutral.

The 'Fake Drake' scare

In early 2023, an anonymous TikTok user released 'Heart on My Sleeve', which used a generative voice model to create vocals that sounded eerily similar to superstars Drake and The Weeknd. The song quickly went viral, racking up millions of views and streams across social media and streaming services. It ignited a global debate around artist identity, copyright infringement and future implications for music production.

While some fans were impressed, industry executives found it alarming due to its implications for copyright infringement and the potential dilution of artists' unique identities.

Universal Music Group, the label for both Drake and The Weeknd, flagged the song to its streaming partners, citing intellectual property concerns. The company also released a statement asking stakeholders in the music ecosystem to choose between supporting artists, fans and human creative expression or supporting deepfakes, fraud and denying artists their due compensation.

The contentious case of 'Fake Drake' serves as an effective lens through which to examine the complexity and range of the ethical concerns stemming from generative AI:

Copyright infringement: AI algorithms are trained on large data sets of existing music, which raises the risk of plagiarism or copyright infringement when AI-generated compositions resemble existing copyrighted works.

Perpetuation of bias: If the algorithms used to generate music are based on data sets that contain biases, the resulting music could reflect those biases, leading to a lack of representation and diversity in the music industry. This issue is of particular concern in the context of cultural and racial appropriation.

Devaluation of human creativity: There are concerns that AI could replace human musicians and producers, leading to job losses and a decrease in the value of human creativity and emotional depth in the music industry. Critics argue that AI music lacks the human touch and soul that defines much of the artistry in music.

The case of 'Fake Drake' highlights the need for clear guidelines for the use of AI in music production, specifically regarding the interplay between copyright and model training data sets. Fortunately, music industry stakeholders and regulators across the US and the European Union are proactively working to update existing frameworks to account for the emergence of generative AI.

Democratisation of music creation

In 2021, 17-year-old David Burke, professionally known as d4vd, grew tired of the constant copyright strikes and takedown notices on his gaming-centric TikTok and YouTube content. Instead of turning to royalty-free background music, d4vd looked up 'how to make music on iPhone'.

He quickly discovered BandLab, a user-friendly, social music creation platform, which has amassed tens of millions of users since its inception in 2015. One of the key features of BandLab is SongStarter, a generative AI tool designed to create musical ideas, including beats, melodies and chord progressions, which can then be built upon via the integrated BandLab production suite.

d4vd used his Apple headphones and the quiet of his sister's closet to record his voice. Then he leveraged BandLab's SongStarter tool to complement his singing with AI-generated music. His music and inspiring story continued to spread across social media until the 2022 release of 'Romantic Homicide'.

The gloomy break-up song went viral, reaching #33 on the Billboard Hot 100 and resulting in a major record label deal with Interscope/Darkroom Records. As of writing, d4vd is among the Top 200 most streamed artists in the world.

d4vd's success is certainly an outlier, yet it exemplifies how generative AI has significantly lowered the barrier to music production. In short, AI enables anyone to make professional-sounding music, even without access to the expensive equipment and expertise that is usually required.

Since its release, BandLab's AI tools have seen significant growth in usage, with the platform reporting a 15x growth in the amount of music being created using its AI tools in 12 months. This growth reflects mainstream excitement around a lower barrier to music creation, but it is not without its existential risks. Mainly, it threatens to dilute, overwhelm and potentially break the open music streaming model.

Spotify currently estimates that 120 000 new songs are added to its platform each day, but only a small number of those songs will receive a singular stream. As more creators discover generative AI tools, streaming catalogues will become diluted, making original creations harder to find and potentially altering the vitally important emotional connection provided by original music.

Not surprisingly, Spotify recently removed thousands of songs that were generated on the Boomy AI platform.

Streaming services are being urged by music industry stakeholders to block AI-generated tracks that rely on copyrighted training data. Adaptive AI may provide a solution once again by identifying and properly attributing AI-generated music, using creation-source metadata to ensure that artists are compensated for their work. However, these methods are still in their early stages and there are many challenges to overcome, including technical issues, legal complexities, and the need for industry-wide standards and practices.

AI: Music's double-edged sword

Disruptive technology has once again left the music industry at an inflection point. Will artificial intelligence usher in the next era of prosperity akin to the CD boom, or will it be a destructive second-coming of Napster?

The answer is not so simple.

AI is already deeply embedded in the creator and consumer ecosystems. ML models have been a core component in satisfying consumer demand and powering the streaming era for more than a decade. Personalised recommendation engines and NLP-powered search functions have let listeners seamlessly navigate nearly limitless catalogues of music.

Without these tools, who knows if streaming platforms would have been able to save the industry from piracy?

Building on those experiences, generative AI is also now becoming a vital step in the creative process. Songwriters are leveraging AI tools as idea generators for lyrics, chords and melodies. Generative AI can easily simulate completed versions of a song without backing musicians. Producers are relying on AI to dissect audio files and isolate specific sounds, experiment with more mixing styles and speed up mundane processes.

For many artists, producers and writers, generative AI is quickly becoming a personal music partner.

Professionals are not the only ones reaping the benefits of generative music AI. Platforms like Boomy and BandLab have empowered their users to create professional-sounding music with no prior music experience. Users can quickly generate instrumentals using short prompts, emojis or preset genres.

As the average amount of time spent on content creation continues to rapidly grow among younger generations, generative AI will play an increasingly important role in satisfying consumer demand for remixed tracks (such as slowed and reverbed versions on TikTok), royalty-free backing music and customised sounds. Generative AI platforms have solidified their place as important creator tools able to serve the entire spectrum of music fans and creators.

But there is another edge to the AI sword.

The pot of royalties distributed by streaming platforms is not growing fast enough to accommodate the increase in content that has been heavily facilitated by generative AI. Career musicians are finding it harder than ever to cut through the noise and generate material income from streaming platforms. The existing economics of the open streaming model does not work for many creators, and industry stakeholders are already feeling the effects of this content glut on their bottom lines.

At the same time, the music industry is racing to develop a training data licensing framework that respects intellectual property laws, while also providing new monetisation opportunities. Fortunately, regulators across the EU and the US are generally aligned with music industry stakeholders and are taking a proactive approach towards emerging technology legislation.

So, will the industry evolve to continue harnessing the power of adaptive and generative artificial intelligence, or will it once again resist until forced to capitulate?

I believe that the music industry has mobilised early enough to be able to get ahead of the potentially destructive power of generative AI, and ride its wave, rather than be swept away.

CHAPTER 16

The AI Future: What Happens Next?

It is now a given that artificial intelligence and machine learning will transform numerous industries, along with the customer experience of banking, insurance and travel services. However, the technology is still in its infancy in terms of clarity of its use cases.

Even the creators of AI and ML platforms and tools have little idea how their resources will be used by innovators – among both start-ups and long-established companies looking for the proverbial better mousetrap.

That is not a bad thing: it means that future applications of AI are limited only by the ability to imagine how they can be used. It also makes possible countless inventive ways of tackling the challenges facing humanity.

It starts with one word.

The secret of tech innovation is not the tech

In property investment, goes the old saying, there are only three criteria: 1. Location. 2. Location. 3. Location.

Innovation in technology can boast an equivalent set of rules, and these are: 1. People. 2. People. 3. People.

Of course, it is more nuanced than that. Tim Ellis, executive for integrated solutions at homegrown South African technology giant Altron, gave me another perspective.

In parallel with people, he told me, the essential elements were: 1. Skills. 2. Skills. 3. Skills.

We were chatting in a coffee shop in the Johannesburg suburb of Linden, ironically directly opposite a government school.

'Mostly, the tech is in place and the platforms we use are already developed. Now it's largely about maintaining and running those systems. And it's critical that the people who maintain those platforms have the right skills. If they don't, we cannot provide that service to our customers.'

Ellis hastened to point out that AI and the ready-made platforms were not the final word in innovation, merely the foundations on which current innovation was being built.

'We are in a platform economy, and there are going to be many more platforms. But with the traditional platforms, even a transport platform like Uber, you're not looking at reinventing them but rather at how you manage, monitor or monetise them.

'In the space that I work in, predominantly around workforce management and smart manufacturing, equivalent platforms are there. And our innovation is around maximising the use of those existing platforms.'

This is particularly true of one of the most arcane areas of technology practice, namely DevOps, typically defined as a set of practices that combine software development and IT operations. It offers a holy grail of innovation in terms of shortening development time and providing continuous delivery and improvement of software – at high quality.

'In the DevOps world, we see more and more entities wanting to grow and build their own applications, and that's an ongoing challenge,' said Ellis. 'You know, applications today are not the apps of years past when you said you're going to need this in two months' time or in six months' time. Instead, it's a never-ending cycle.'

Without the right people in place, and those people equipped with the right skills, DevOps is dead in the water. That, in turn, means that a company falls behind the innovation curve and, more significantly, behind its competitors.

'If you look at most of the large banks, they have always had a legacy environment. Going back many years, it was based on IBM. But that is changing at a rapid rate, as our customers have now moved those applications into the cloud. You need a DevOps team to do that migration or that modernisation. As a result, the DevOps individuals and teams that can provide this service are critical to growth.'

Many organisations still operate on traditional development cycles, needs and priorities. However, even those holdouts cannot ignore the importance of utilising AI and big data, the large and complex data sets produced by their activities, customers and applications. Only by using AI to analyse their own big data can they successfully deliver innovations that meet customer needs.

'The important thing is we've now moved into a data-driven economy. Everything is about data. Most people understand that if you do a search on Google for something, you're going to be bombarded with whatever you were searching. But banks rely on the data that they get; medical aids rely on that data to make the next decision for the business, but also for what they're going to provide for their customers.'

Ellis made a controversial suggestion that emphasised the importance of people over technology: 'The Fourth Industrial Revolution is a dated concept. Now it's about people and their data, and how you manage or manipulate that data. That is what's driving this economy, as well as individual companies.'

The ordinary power of AI

Clearly, it is dawning on the business world that AI is not only about robots taking away jobs and taking over the world. More often, it is about running our businesses and our lives more efficiently.

As more businesses discover the very ordinary power of AI to help them do extraordinary things, the demand for this power grows. For many, however, AI seems inaccessible, due to lack of skills or the high cost of solutions.

Enter Zindi, a Cape Town-based start-up, established in 2018 with the aim of making data science and AI skills accessible to companies in Africa. It literally crowdsourced AI, inviting companies to post a challenge on its site and posing the challenge to a community of more than 40 000 data scientists from across the continent. This meant companies could get hundreds of talented data scientists working on their problem – at low cost.

'We created Zindi because we recognised that there was this gap in the market,' co-founder and CEO Celina Lee told me. 'The amount of data that companies in Africa and around the world are generating is growing exponentially. They are getting really excited about AI and data science, but a lot of them don't know how to start.'

This meant the demand was there, but part of not knowing where to start was the perceived shortage of skills in South Africa and across Africa. This was the real gap that Zindi spotted.

'People are coming out of the continent who have the raw talent to be data scientists. They're just looking for the chance to connect with the opportunities to showcase their capabilities and to hone their skills on real business problems. We wanted to make space for these two sides to find each other, for young people to find opportunities and for companies to find the talent.'

Since 2018, Zindi initially expanded to Kenya and the UK. By 2023, the 40 000 data scientists on the platform represented 150 countries, with 45 in Africa, representing 70% of the participants.

'It's amazing that people from India, Latin America, the Middle East and Eastern Europe are coming to the platform as well. We've run over 100 challenges on the platform, and each of these represents a real-world problem that the community came together to solve,' Lee said.

The clients ranged from global tech giants like Microsoft, Google and AWS to telcos and financial service providers, all the way down to start-ups. It was revealing that world leaders in AI and ML were using the platform, given that they were themselves creating platforms for others to develop AI and ML solutions.

'They have their data science teams, they have the top technology in the world, but they see value in the talent that's on the platform. They recognise that Africa has the fastest growing working-age population in the world. So, a lot of these global tech players are coming to us and to the continent, because they are looking to connect with the unseen talent that is now being uncovered by players like Zindi.'

A prime example was AWS running a challenge for the South African National Space Agency (SANSA) to use ML to analyse informal settlements in the country.

'While AWS wanted to provide support for that kind of use case, SANSA being one of their partners, it was important for them as a company to access talent.

'What has ended up happening is that by building this community we're also bringing together talent in a way that has never happened before. Everyone's looking for data scientists, and Zindi is providing a community for every African data scientist in one place, which provides opportunities for them and also opportunities for companies.'

Why we don't need Sophia the Robot

Do you have time for another flashback?

In 2019, some months after the South African president, Cyril Ramaphosa, had appointed a presidential commission on the Fourth Industrial Revolution to recommend policies and strategies, the topic was debated in the South African parliament. The then deputy president, David Mabuza, was asked what the first three industrial revolutions entailed. He described it as a 'new question' and said: 'I am not very sure as a country whether we are in the third industrial revolution or second industrial revolution.'

It gets worse.

In the same week, it was announced that a robot would headline the annual government technology conference called GovTech. The disconnect between government knowledge and government marketing about its knowledge could not have been starker.

Hosted by the State Information Technology Agency (SITA), the event, held in Durban, explored how technology and ICT infrastructure development would digitally transform and uplift various sectors. It's official theme was 'Digital Transformation: Gearing towards the Fourth Industrial Revolution (4IR) and beyond'.

However, using Sophia the Robot as the symbol of 4IR was probably as big a faux pas as leaders not being able to explain the first three industrial revolutions or define the fourth.

'She' was really a public relations exercise by AI firm Hanson Robotics to show off its engineering brilliance. Able to display more than 50 facial expressions, it was as close to mimicking human gesture and expression as a robot had ever come.

Its creators pulled off a masterstroke of marketing in 2017 when they persuaded the Saudi Arabian government to grant citizenship to Sophia. It was a bitter irony: it gave a robot woman almost more rights than real female citizens of that country.

When Sophia visited South Africa for the first time in 2018, I was invited to put questions to her. However, the organisers provided me with sample questions in advance. When I submitted my own questions instead, the interview was cancelled.

That could well have been a result of logistics, but it did not help dispel the notion that Sophia's artificial intelligence was really just a matter of building a chatbot into a machine with a face.

In other words, Sophia's brain was no more advanced than the voice assistant on a standard iPhone or Android smartphone. The difference is that we only got to hear Sophia talk from a stage, whereas we can talk to Apple Siri or Google Assistant or Huawei Celia anytime, anywhere.

Why was this a problem? Hanson Robotics stated the issue quite eloquently: 'She personifies our dreams for the future of AI. As a unique combination of science, engineering and artistry, Sophia is simultaneously a human-crafted science fiction character depicting the future of AI and robotics, and a platform for advanced robotics and AI research.'

No, it's not.

Casting Sophia in this light put the government's 4IR strategy in perspective: it revealed it to be more of a public relations exercise than a truly transformative strategy. It explained why we heard much cheerleading from government for 4IR, but little of substance.

The work being done by the Urology Hospital in Pretoria in using robotic assistants for surgery, or by Mitchell Designs in Bloemfontein to manufacture low-cost prosthetics and EvansWerks in Cape Town to produce prototype designs on demand, both using 3D printers, is far more relevant to 4IR than any of this hype.

The pioneering work being done by Cape Town's Aerobotics in using drones and AI for agriculture is far more transformative than Sophia the Robot. Johannesburg-based Naked Insurance is using more AI to generate instant quotes and payments than we saw in action during every GovTech conference ever held.

The real Fourth Industrial Revolution is already happening, despite our leaders, rather than thanks to them.

Fortunately, this may be changing. In an interview in October 2023 with Dr Bongani Mabaso, the new CEO of SITA, he told me that his top priority was to return the organisation to its original mandate, with a threefold imperative:

- Focus on public services, in other words e-services that citizens actually want to use;
- Efficiency, by automating basic backend services and providing reliable, cost-effective solutions with a quick turnaround time; and
- Increasing cyber-resilience across government.

Mabaso, whose doctorate happens to be in artificial intelligence, believes AI can play a big role in SITA's service delivery. He sees it 'supporting service delivery, citizen convenience, automation of routine and complex processes at the back, as well as providing new experiences in which citizens can experience government service delivery'.

AI and the new cybersecurity arms race

And now for the bad news. I mean, more bad news.

Thanks to generative AI tools, a new cybersecurity arms race has broken out across the world.

The ready availability of services like ChatGPT and Bing Image Creator have enhanced the ability of scammers to create hoax news reports, images, sounds and videos. These allow cybercriminals to steal identities to commit financial fraud or create more convincing phishing campaigns aimed at getting users to click on malicious links that expose them to malware, ransomware and data breaches.

Just how sophisticated the scammers get was first revealed to me at a conference hosted by global cybersecurity provider Kaspersky in Almaty, Kazakhstan, in May 2023. It was announced there by the firm's Global Research and Analysis Team that South Africa had seen a 14% increase in users exposed to phishing attacks in the first three months of 2023, compared to the last quarter of 2022.

Nigeria had seen a 17% increase in such attacks and Egypt 53%, indicating the potential scope for the escalation of cybercrime across Africa.

While these attacks were not a direct result of generative AI, they indicated the potential escalation of cybercrime across the continent.

Vladislav Tushkanov, lead data scientist at Kaspersky, told the conference that three separate categories of generative AI were already being used in scams:

- **Diffusion networks**, a type of AI that can generate any kind of image from a text description by learning patterns from existing examples and then using those patterns to generate similar material. The best-known examples at the time of writing were Midjourney, Microsoft Bing Image Creator and Stable Diffusion.
- **Deepfakes**, which insert people's faces into videos and animate still portraits. DeepFaceLab was a leader in the field.
- **Large language models**, which generate any kind of text and solve text-based problems.

'These technologies have a bright side but also a dark side. Each technology can bring value for business but also introduce vulnerabilities and enable cybercriminals,' said Tushkanov.

He gave examples of a British energy company being breached using voice deepfakes to impersonate employees and the US government issuing an official warning that deepfakes were being used to apply for remote jobs. And those came well before the current generative AI explosion began.

More recently, in September 2022, deepfake videos were made of Elon Musk endorsing a cryptocurrency scam. It was so effective that he had to announce on Twitter that it was 'Defs not me'.

Said Tushkanov: 'It turned out, through our research, that deepfakes were being sold on the darknet (a version of the web accessible only through specialised browsers) for many use cases, including creating advertisements for crypto scams and harassment on social media.'

Later, I asked Tushkanov to elaborate.

'This technology is still very basic,' he said. 'Right now, it only generates images over which you have almost no control. But they are getting better and better because we have much more computational resources, we have faster graphics processors and better hardware, so we can generate better images and videos.

'You will be able to generate a picture of any person at any time, in any environment. It can be captivating, and it can draw attention, but then it can also be used by cybercriminals.'

Most significantly, the technologies are becoming simpler to use.

'A year ago, creating a nice picture wasn't as simple. You couldn't just log into a web interface and create. You had to have some basic computer skills. Now, as they become more accessible, more of these low-level campaigns might employ them. It's not there yet, but it's coming.'

The warning echoed Microsoft chief economist Michael Schwarz, talking on a World Economic Forum panel in Geneva at the same time. He said AI could help make humans more productive and revolutionise the way most businesses operate, but 'guardrails' had to be erected.

'I am confident AI will be used by bad actors, and, yes, it will cause real damage,' he said. 'It can do a lot of damage in the hands of spammers with elections and so on.'

Craig Rosewarne, MD of South African cybersecurity consultancy Wolfpack Information Risk, gave me some good news: 'We've seen that criminals are still not as tech-savvy operating in South Africa. Generally, we see it more coming from the Western African regions and some attacks coming in from Eastern Europe.

'We are starting to see more cybercrime-as-a-service being used, where you've got the whole underground economy operating together, where some people use a platform for launching ransomware or denial-of-service attacks that get rented out. But watch this space. We're going to start seeing a lot more of it happening.

'We saw IBM recently announcing a layoff of about 30% of its non-client-facing workforce. So, as companies are starting to adopt and use AI, obviously cybercriminals are going to start to use it more and more.

'ChatGPT still has safeguards built into it, so if you ask it to go find security vulnerabilities on the Wolfpack website, it will say that it cannot do it. But, of course, there are ways of posing questions, for example, asking how would you go about doing it?

'If we compare it to the iPhone, it's at the iPhone 1 stage. Of course, we're now sitting on iPhone 15. With this, it's going to just multiply dramatically, so big things are coming.'

That means there is still time for the business world to prepare.

Tushkanov said the answer, for now, was not technology but awareness: 'Understanding how AI changes the world and educating the public about AI is of utmost importance.'

AI changes everything

'Artificial intelligence changes everything.' With that opening statement in his keynote address at the Oracle CloudWorld conference in Las Vegas in September 2023, Oracle founder and chairperson Larry Ellison set the tone for the biggest shift in strategy for the software business since the arrival of the personal computer. And it will have a profound impact on business and consumers.

'Generative AI is a revolution, a breakthrough, fundamentally changing things at Oracle,' he said. 'This makes AI central to almost everything we're doing and fundamentally changes how we build applications, run applications; it changes everything.

'Is generative AI the most important new computer technology ever? Probably. One thing is for certain – we will find out, because countless billions of dollars are being invested in generative AI and language models.'

The second biggest software company in the world after Microsoft, Oracle is the market leader in database systems, processing more business and customer data than any other organisation. This gives it a first-hand view of change as it happens. Oracle itself unveiled new AI capabilities across most of its products and services. And it was highly specific in the impact these will have on day-to-day activity.

The Oracle Fusion suite of cloud-based applications, for example, will include a wide range of new AI capabilities for improving customer experience:

- 'Assisted authoring' will help customer service representatives write responses to customers more quickly and accurately.
- 'Assisted knowledge' will help document standard operating procedures for complex problems more quickly and accurately.
- 'Search augmentation' will help employees find the best solution to a customer's question more quickly.
- Customer engagement summaries will summarise the history of communications with a customer for customer service representatives who are new to the case.
- AI-suggested troubleshooting content will help technicians in the field to resolve problems more quickly and efficiently.

Richard Smith, Oracle executive vice-president for technology across Europe, the Middle East and Africa, told me that there were several fundamental differences in the way AI is being embraced in Western markets compared to countries like South Africa.

'There are varying degrees of adoption,' he said. 'If you look across some of the larger regions, in North America right now there are significant funding levels and companies making significant and major commercial AI bets. In African countries and the Middle East, the governments are driving AI agendas or looking to strongly support them in a spirit of innovation for the country. Some of those are quite mature and some of them not so much.

'A lot of the time, when I'm visiting a region or making a call on a public sector customer, I'm asked how I can help both in terms of providing capacity and providing intelligence and support in that space. A lot of customers are asking, "What do I do with it? What should I do with it? Do I need to touch it at all?" The winners are going to be the people who ask the best questions.'

Smith said he talked to many banks, including those in South Africa, at a very senior level.

'What they tell me is, "I'm a good bank – 90% of what I do is consistent with what my competition does. How can I use AI to define and innovate against that remaining 10% so that it creates a better set of services versus my competition and grows my organisation?" How they can be better and be more efficient is the type of question starting to emerge industry by industry by industry. That will start to morph into things that are very, very good for the world, from a commercial standpoint, from a personal and from a social welfare standpoint.'

The most intensive activity, however, was not coming from large organisations, said Smith.

'We see across your region a very high propensity of start-ups, small groups of companies, small groups of people, experimenting with AI. That is often industry-driven, whether it's a healthcare question, whether it's around government or digital services. Right now, there is massive activity, but the overwhelming focus is where you just get a group of very smart people who say, "Look, we have this capability, we have this learning model, what can we do?" That to me, is where the excitement starts to come up.'

In many cases, the impact of AI will not be obvious to the ordinary person in the street, but the benefits will be dramatic, especially in healthcare. Oracle is heavily focused on the sector and last year made its biggest acquisition yet, buying the electronic health records firm Cerner for $28.3 billion.

'The question was, "Hang on, you're a cloud technology provider, why are you buying a healthcare company? Why is that important?" Larry's view is that you can use data, AI and machine learning to identify, for example, the next pathogen before it occurs, and do so at speed. If you can use AI to identify oncology patterns, you can individualise cancer treatments for individuals based on genomic sequencing.'

During a panel discussion at CloudWorld, Mike Sicilia, executive vice-president of Oracle Global Industries, said that other sectors would also see dramatic advances.

'If you think about retail business and hospitality business and food and beverage, the customer loyalty scenario can really be enhanced with everyday customer outreach. All these things can be personalised, based on buying patterns, based on interaction patterns. I don't think there's an industry that is not affected. There's an application or use cases across every industry.'

Ellison himself neatly summed up the significance of generative AI of the kind that was launched by ChatGPT in November 2022 and sparked the current AI frenzy: 'ChatGPT has captured our imagination. Most new technology does not capture the attention of heads of state. This is like the Sputnik moment.'

Back in the RSA

A $4-billion investment announced at the end of September by AWS into Anthropic, one of the hottest AI start-ups in the world, set the scene for the next phase in the generative AI race.

While AWS will become Anthropic's cloud computing provider, the start-up will also have access to the cloud giant's full compute infrastructure, referring to the services that provide processing power in the cloud. AWS already ran a platform called Amazon Bedrock, which made third-party AI models like Claude, Anthropic's rival to ChatGPT, available to its customers.

South African-born David Brown, senior vice-president of AWS Compute, was in Johannesburg for an AWS Summit at the time of the announcement. He told me that the deal would be of great significance to South Africa and the rest of the continent.

'Generative AI is definitely going to play a role in Africa. Our focus is about price performance. It's about, how do I get more performance for every rand that I spend? That's going to be key to developing markets.

'You're not going to have a business that can afford some of the levels of investments [in AI] that you've seen from some of these really big players. We don't have enough venture funds in some of these developing countries, so we've got to innovate like crazy on the [AI] models. We have to innovate on the hardware, make services available that can allow businesses within developing countries like South Africa to take advantage of these things. It's something that they can say, "Hey, I can deploy this thing and it can make my customers' lives better."'

Brown was part of the team that built the original AWS cloud, known as EC2, at a Cape Town development centre from 2004 to 2006. It kicked off the global cloud computing revolution, and it set the company on a trajectory to becoming Amazon's most profitable division. In 2022, it contributed $80 billion to revenue and $23 billion in operating profit.

During the AWS Summit, Brown told more than 4 000 delegates that the Cape Town team never imagined the impact they would make.

'There's been so much learning and breakthrough since those early years, and we've only accelerated our pace of innovation.'

Chris Erasmus, South African country manager of AWS, told me on the sidelines of the AWS Summit that there was massive interest in the Anthropic investment and its ChatGPT rival Claude.

'In South Africa, there is huge interest already, specifically in financial services. A lot of the financial services institutions are looking at use cases. They are already starting to run proofs of concept leveraging the likes of Amazon Bedrock. That will be the key industry that we will see the most progress in quite early. Other organisations look to financial services to be the ones to essentially make it safe and secure.

'Once they are solved for something, it becomes easy for everyone else to adopt it.'

South Africa must commit to the future

During a visit to South Africa in October 2023, Chuck Robbins, CEO of global networking hardware leader Cisco Systems, told me in an interview that, in order to drive growth and prosperity, the country must drive connectivity and digitalisation of services. During his visit, Cisco announced the launch of a second Country Digital Acceleration (CDA) programme in South Africa. The first, initiated in September 2019, saw Cisco invest $9.2 million in IT job creation, skills and talent development, and national cybersecurity.

The aim: 'to build sustainable, secure, and inclusive communities powered by ethical and innovative technology solutions'.

'You have to fundamentally believe that it's going to be good for the economy,' Robbins told me. 'If you believe that, you'll make the investments. Once [the population is] connected, you can deliver education, you can deliver aspects of healthcare, people can now work from wherever they are in certain jobs. So, it really opens up huge opportunity when we get everyone connected.'

While he would not be drawn on specific reasons for South Africa falling behind in the evolution of digital government, he said that the issue usually came down to one word: 'commitment'.

'You just have to gain conviction on that,' he said. 'And you have to believe that. Countries have to look at public-private partnerships, where it's so important for the infrastructure in the country to be built out, and whether that's going to be done by private carriers or private telecommunications companies. Sometimes it may require a public-private partnership to make those investments, to get that core foundation built, because it's the backbone of the digital economy.'

He said AI would play a major role in Cisco's technology, and it was likely to make ongoing product announcements in that regard.

I asked him why we should be excited about AI, and he gave one of the most practical and positive summaries I've heard from an executive: 'Artificial intelligence has the potential to solve some of the biggest problems in the world. It has the potential to help us solve water supply issues. Food supply issues. It can help us solve the speed at which we can diagnose diseases with doctors. Think about using artificial intelligence to digest massive amounts of historical healthcare data, and correlate that with what a doctor is seeing today in a patient, and then have the doctor first assess and make sure that the assumptions and the conclusions are accurate, but then be able to prescribe and get that patient on the journey to health faster. That's one use case that is going to be very powerful and there's so many of these that we're very excited about.'

Did he expect AI to have an impact on addressing the challenges faced by every country across the African continent?

'Well, it certainly can,' he said. 'It's dependent upon getting the core infrastructure built out, getting core connectivity built out, and bringing people onto the Internet, so that we can provide education, prepare them for the next-generation jobs. Then, ultimately, AI can certainly play an important role in the future development of the continent.'

The future is ready for us: Are we ready for the future?

I part with a thought that is repeated several times in this book: in Silicon Valley, innovation is driven by opportunity; across Africa, it is driven by need.

The immediate future, let's say from 2024 to 2028, is being built today. By 2030, the world will be a very different place, politically, socially, economically and technologically. There is little doubt that technology will help make many of the bad things worse, and many of the good things better. It will provide an enabling environment for those who want to use it both for self-enrichment and for betterment of the world.

AI will be at the heart of many of the coming changes, especially when it is built into everyday, affordable and pervasive devices.

In this future, the opportunity for innovation will be unprecedented. There will be room for those who want to do things in old or traditional ways, but the world will be changed by those who embrace this future.

As has always been the case, not everyone has equal access to this future. The digital divide between rich and poor, developed and undeveloped, educated and uneducated may well be widened by AI.

The best comment I've heard summing up this scenario is from one of my favourite authors, William Gibson, who coined the word 'cyberspace' in his science fiction novel *Neuromancer*. He said: 'The future is already here – it's just not very evenly distributed.'[1]

That comment contains many layers of meaning, and it allows us to delve into the nature of the digital divide between the industrialised and developing worlds, urban and rural populations, and resource-rich and resource-poor people and populations.

AI will indeed be unevenly distributed, but it is also pregnant with the potential for smoothing out that distribution. Particularly in developing countries like those on the African continent, many will not only recognise but also exuberantly embrace that potential in seeking to address the challenges of their environments.

The future is ready for us, and we must be ready for the future.

Notes

Chapter 1 When AI Was Young

1 Jonathan Swift, *Gulliver's Travels*. London: Penguin, 2001 [1726].

Chapter 2: World, Meet AI

1 Arthur Goldstuck, 'Generative AI Will Soon be the Bedrock of Business', *Sunday Times*, 18 June 2023, https://www.timeslive.co.za/sunday-times/business/business/2023-06-18-generative-ai-will-soon-be-the-bedrock-of-business/.

2 Kirsten Grieshaber, 'Can a Chatbot Preach a Good Sermon? Hundreds Attend Church Service Generated by ChatGPT to Find out', *Associated Press*, 10 June 2023, https://apnews.com/article/germany-church-protestants-chatgpt-ai-sermon.

3 Carlos Bajo Erro, 'The Entrepreneur Who Wants to Decolonize Artificial Intelligence in Africa', *El País*, 9 October 2023, https://english.elpais.com/technology/2023-10-09/the-entrepreneur-who-wants-to-decolonize-artificial-intelligence-in-africa.html.

4 https://lelapa.ai/.

Chapter 4: The Art of the Prompt

1 University of Pretoria, 'Guide for ChatGPT Usage in Teaching and Learning', 2023, https://www.up.ac.za/media/shared/391/pdfs/up-guide-for-chatgtp-for-teaching-and-learning.zp233629.pdf.

2 https://digitalstrategies.tuck.dartmouth.edu/wp-content/uploads/2023/04/ChatGPT-Cheat-Sheet.pdf.

3 https://www.kdnuggets.com/publications/sheets/ChatGPT_Cheatsheet_Costa.pdf.

4 https://www.codecademy.com/learn/intro-to-chatgpt/modules/prompt-engineering-with-chat-gpt/cheatsheet.

Chapter 6: Before AI Gets Down to Business

1 Mark L. Grabe, Colene Byrne and Doug Johnston, 'The Impact of Electronic Health Records on Diagnosis', *Diagnosis* 4(4), https://doi.org/10.1515/dx-2017-0012.

2 Jeffrey Dastin, 'Amazon Scraps Secret AI Recruiting Tool that Showed Bias against Women', *Reuters*, 11 October 2018, https://www.reuters.com/article/us-amazon-com-jobs-automation-insight-idUSKCN1MK08G.

Chapter 7: AI Means Business

1 Arthur Goldstuck, 'Glimpse of the Future has Audience Gasping', *BusinessLive*, 3 December 2017, https://www.businesslive.co.za/bt/business-and-economy/2017-12-03-arthur-goldstuck-glimpse-of-the-future-has-audience-gasping/.
2 June Yang and Burak Gokturk, 'Google Cloud Brings Generative AI to Developers, Businesses, and Government', *Google Cloud*, 14 March 2023, https://cloud.google.com/blog/products/ai-machine-learning/generative-ai-for-businesses-and-governments.
3 Eduardo Baptista and Josh Ye, 'China's Answer to ChatGPT? Baidu Shares Tumble as Ernie Bot Disappoints', *Reuters*, 16 March 2023, https://www.reuters.com/technology/chinese-search-giant-baidu-introduces-ernie-bot-2023-03-16/.

Chapter 9: My Doctor, the Machine

1 https://www.gov.za/faq/health/what-are-leading-causes-death-south-africa.

Chapter 10: AI Hits the Road

1 William J. McGee, 'How to Get the Lowest Airfares', *Consumer Reports*, 25 August 2016, https://www.consumerreports.org/airline-travel/how-to-get-the-lowest-airfares/.

Chapter 11: AI Wants to Make Things

1 Deloitte, 'Leading the Social Enterprise: Reinvent with a Human Focus', 2019, https://www2.deloitte.com/content/dam/insights/us/articles/5136_HC-Trends-2019/DI_HC-Trends-2019.pdf.
2 http://www.worldwideworx.com/4ir/.

Chapter 12: When the Going Gets Tough, AI Goes Shopping

1 Greg Linden, Brent Smith and Jeremy York, 'Amazon.com Recommendations: Item-to-Item Collaborative Filtering', *IEEE Internet Computing*, 2003, http://www.cs.umd.edu/~samir/498/Amazon-Recommendations.pdf.
2 Larry Hardesty, 'The History of Amazon's Recommendation Algorithm', *Amazon Science*, 22 November 2019, https://www.amazon.science/the-history-of-amazons-recommendation-algorithm.
3 Jay Peters, '"Every Single" Amazon Team Is Working on Generative AI, Says CEO', *The Verge*, 4 August 2023, https://www.theverge.com/2023/8/3/23819442/amazon-generative-ai-ceo.
4 Linden, Smith and York, 'Amazon.com Recommendations'.
5 Danilo Poccia, 'Amazon Forecast – Time Series Forecasting Made Easy', *AWS*, 28 November 2018, https://aws.amazon.com/blogs/aws/amazon-forecast-time-series-forecasting-made-easy/.

6 Stuart Lauchlan, 'Dreamforce 2023 – "We Call Them Hallucinations; I Call them Lies!" Benioff's Call to Arms around the Generative AI Trust Gap', *Diginomica*, 12 September 2023, https://diginomica.com/dreamforce-2023-we-call-them-hallucinations-i-call-them-lies-benioffs-call-arms-around-generative.
7 Pragati Gupta, 'ChatGPT Prompts for E-Commerce: Upgrade Your E-Commerce Marketing in 2023', *Writesonic*, 29 April 2023, https://writesonic.com/blog/chatgpt-prompts-ecommerce.
8 https://aihabit.net/chatgpt-prompts-for-ecommerce.

Chapter 13: That Will Teach the AI

1 Neil Postman, *Technopoly: The Surrender of Culture to Technology*. New York: Alfred A. Knopf, 1992.
2 Stephen Marche, 'The College Essay Is Dead', *The Atlantic*, 6 December 2022, https://www.theatlantic.com/technology/archive/2022/12/chatgpt-ai-writing-college-student-essays/672371/.
3 Mike Sharples, 'New AI Tools That Can Write Student Essays Require Educators to Rethink Teaching and Assessment' *LSE*, 17 May 2022, https://blogs.lse.ac.uk/impactofsocialsciences/2022/05/17/new-ai-tools-that-can-write-student-essays-require-educators-to-rethink-teaching-and-assessment/.
4 Dan Rosenzweig-Ziff, 'New York City Blocks Use of the ChatGPT Bot in Its Schools', *The Washington Post*, 5 January 2023, https://www.washingtonpost.com/education/2023/01/05/nyc-schools-ban-chatgpt/.
5 Michael Elsen-Rooney, 'NYC Education Department Blocks ChatGPT on School Devices, Networks', *Chalkbeat*, 4 January 2023, https://ny.chalkbeat.org/2023/1/3/23537987/nyc-schools-ban-chatgpt-writing-artificial-intelligence.
6 https://teaching.washington.edu/course-design/chatgpt/.
7 Kalley Huang, 'Alarmed by AI Chatbots, Start Revamping How They Teach', *The New York Times*, 16 January 2023, https://www.nytimes.com/2023/01/16/technology/chatgpt-artificial-intelligence-universities.html.
8 Huang, 'Alarmed by AI Chatbots'.
9 Marc Allen Cu and Sebastian Hockman, 'Scores of Stanford Students Used ChatGPT on Final Exams, Survey Suggests', *The Stanford Daily*, 22 January 2023, https://stanforddaily.com/2023/01/22/scores-of-stanford-students-used-chatgpt-on-final-exams-survey-suggests/#:~:text=%E2%80%9CStudents%20are%20expected%20to%20complete,OpenAI%20and%20launched%20in%20November.
10 https://www.plagiarism.admin.cam.ac.uk/what-academic-misconduct/artificial-intelligence.
11 Theo Baker, 'Stanford President Resigns over Manipulated Research, Will Retract at Least Three Papers', *The Stanford Daily*, 19 July 2023, https://stanforddaily.com/2023/07/19/stanford-president-resigns-over-manipulated-research-will-retract-at-least-3-papers/.
12 University of Pretoria, 'Guide for ChatGPT Usage in Teaching and Learning', 2023, https://www.up.ac.za/media/shared/391/pdfs/up-guide-for-chatgtp-for-teaching-and-learning.zp233629.pdf.
13 Rahem D. Hamid and Elias J. Schisgall, 'CS50 Will Integrate Artificial Intelligence into Course Instruction', *The Harvard Crimson*, 21 June 2023, https://www.thecrimson.com/article/2023/6/21/cs50-artificial-intelligence/.

Chapter 14: Feed the AI, Feed the Planet

1 https://habana.ai/about-us/#:~:text=We%20are%20unlocking%20the%20true,as%20an%20independent%20Intel%20company.
2 https://aws.amazon.com/solutions/case-studies/aerobotics-case-study/.
3 https://www.oracle.com/za/news/announcement/people-believe-bots-will-succeed-where-humans-have-failed-2022-04-20/.
4 Melissa Evatt, 'Business Leaders Back Bots to Bolster ESG Efforts', *ERP Today*, 29 April 2022, https://erp.today/business-leaders-back-bots-to-bolster-esg-efforts/.

Chapter 15: The AI Future of Music

1 Alex Suskind, '15 Years after Napster: How the Music Service Changed the Industry', *Daily Beast*, 12 July 2017, https://www.thedailybeast.com/15-years-after-napster-how-the-music-service-changed-the-industry#:~:text=Since%20then%2C%20Napster%20has%20gone,%2C%20to%20name%20a%20few).
2 https://engineering.atspotify.com/2020/01/for-your-ears-only-personalizing-spotify-home-with-machine-learning/.
3 Chris Garcia, 'Algorithmic Music – David Cope and EMI', *CHM*, 29 April 2015, https://computerhistory.org/blog/algorithmic-music-david-cope-and-emi/#:~:text=%E2%80%9CExperiments%20in%20Musical%20Intelligence%20is,pieces%20exactly.%E2%80%9D%20he%20noted.

Chapter 16: The AI Future: What Happens Next?

1 https://quoteinvestigator.com/2012/01/24/future-has-arrived/.

Acknowledgements

This book would not have been possible without the numerous contributions that went into my fascinating journey over the years as a hitchhiker on the AI travels of so many people, organisations, start-ups and enterprises.

Some of these were fortuitous, but none as fortuitous as a trip up the road from my home when I was invited by writer Terry Shakinovsky to moderate a panel discussion on the future of the book at the Parkview Literary Festival in 2022. On my panel was Terry Morris, MD of Pan Macmillan in South Africa, and I found her to have a profound and practical grasp of the future. This was confirmed by an informal chat afterwards, and I decided she would be the first person I would approach the next time I answered the inner call to write a book.

When my daughter Zianda suggested I write a book on AI, after listening to one of numerous radio and TV interviews I gave on the topic, it took about three seconds to realise that was my next book. Three minutes later, I emailed the suggestion to Terry, and less than a week later I was in her office, where our mutual enthusiasm for the project was shared by Pan Macmillan publisher Andrea Nattrass and associate editor Zodwa Kumalo-Valentine. Subsequently, the delightful minds of Pan Macmillan head of communications Nkanyezi Tshabalala, publicist Shakti Pillay and digital communications coordinator Zenande Bidli entered the fray, building out one of the best brains trusts I have yet worked with on a book. AI cannot compete with either the enthusiasm or the insight of this remarkable team.

Thank you to my editor of the book, Sally Hines, for a gentle but insistent hand on my words (but Sally, I do hanker for the Oxford comma), Jane Bowman for proofreading what must often seem like a new language, and Marius Roux for a wonderful cover that captures the tone of the book so well.

A massive thank you must go to my wife Sheryl, my right hand, my engine room, my manager and my non-AI prompter, for keeping the foundations in place while I was building the walls and roof of a new book. Inspiration also came from Jay, now living in Los Angeles and completing a documentary film at the time of writing. Knowing that there were deadlines playing out at opposite ends of the world kept me focused on keeping my side of the bargain.

My core team at World Wide Worx and Gadget, data analyst Jason Bannier and content manager Angelique Mogotlane, helped me explore the limits of ethical AI across all aspects of the business, contributing to a hands-on understanding of how significant the revolution was going to be for all.

Thank you to the team at the University of the Witwatersrand, with which my twin brother Charles and I are exploring new vistas for researching AI in the real world: Dr Christo Doherty, professor and head of digital arts at the School of Arts; Dr Benji Rosman in the School of Computer Science and Applied Mathematics (who wrote the foreword to the book); Dr Adam Pantanowitz, director of the Wits Innovation Centre; and Dr Lucienne Abrahams, director of the LINK Centre. Our many discussions made a major contribution to fine-tuning the perspectives in this book. Thank you to the vice-chancellor, Professor Zeblon Vilakazi, and the late Professor Barry Dwolatzky, for initiating those conversations. Barry passed away as the book was being conceived, but his contribution will never be forgotten.

The many journalists and producers from TV channels, radio stations, podcasts, online media, newspapers and magazines who interviewed me on the topic over the years helped me hone my thinking, perspectives and forecasts about AI. Thank you and forgive me if I am off hitchhiking again the next time you call me.

Finally, all the communications and public relations teams of all the high-tech organisations – ranging from information technology to sports – that gave me access to their people, projects and events, made possible the hands-on experience of AI that fuels this book.

AI is defined by what it makes possible, but it is people who make AI possible. Thank you, people.